The Professional Vocalist

A HANDBOOK FOR COMMERCIAL SINGERS AND TEACHERS

Rachel L. Lebon

The Scarecrow Press, Inc.
Lanham, Md., & London
1999

SCARECROW PRESS, INC.

Published in the United States of America
by Scarecrow Press, Inc.,
4720 Boston Way, Lanham, Maryland 20706

4 Pleydell Gardens, Folkestone
Kent CT20 2DN, England

Copyright © 1999 by Rachel L. Lebon

British Library Cataloguing in Publication Information Available

Library of Congress Cataloging-in-Publication Data

Lebon, Rachel L., 1951–
    The professional vocalist : a handbook for commercial singers and
teachers / Rachel L. Lebon.
      p. cm.
    Includes bibliographical references and index.
    ISBN 0-8108-3565-7 (alk. paper). — ISBN 0-8108-3566-5 (pbk. :
alk. paper)
    1. Singing—Instruction and study.   2. Singing—Vocational
guidance. I. Title.
MT855.L43   1999
783—dc21   98-30718
                                       CIP
                                       MN

Printed in the United States of America

∞ The paper used in this publication meets the minimum requirements of
American National Standard for Information Sciences—Permanence of
Paper for Printed Library Materials, ANSI Z39.48–1984.

*I dedicate this work to my mother, Mrs. Georgette Lebon,
and in memory of my father, Raymond Joseph Lebon,
without whom none of my "journeys"
would have been possible*

Bel Canto [It.] The Italian vocal technique of the eighteenth century, with its emphasis on beauty of sound and brilliance of performance rather than dramatic expression or romantic emotion.

—HARVARD DICTIONARY OF MUSIC

After all, what is music but pushing air?

—VAL VALENTIN, studio recording engineer for many distinguished singers (including Sinatra, Nat King Cole, Judy Garland, and Ella Fitzgerald), in an interview with Michael Alldred, "Four Decades of Engineering—Engineer Val Valentin Remembers . . .," *Grammy Pulse,* September 1986

From the best singers, I get the feeling somehow that they're spontaneously creating the lyrics as they go because they want to communicate that idea to me; I don't get the feeling that they're singing to show how great they sound. That's one reason that too much training evident in a voice can be a detriment for singing on commercials; people tend to focus on the voice itself rather than the message the voice is meant to convey.

—GARY FRY, Chicago jingle producer (McDonald's, United Airlines, and other major national jingles) and film composer

These three observations represent radically differing perspectives regarding music and the art of singing. While some individuals identify beauty of tone as the sine qua non of artistic singing, others emphasize the ability to be expressive while communicating ideas and feelings with the human voice. Still others are more oriented towards the scientific, technological, and acoustic. The result is a wide gamut of musical and vocal approaches, styles, and idioms that represent individual and unique perspectives of the world in which we live.

CONTENTS

PREFACE

I was performing extensively, in both the classical and pop/jazz idioms, before I had ever had any voice training, with the exception of 6 months of voice with Mother John of the Eucharist, who upon hearing my self-taught version of Strauss's "Voices of Spring" for an audition, promptly assigned me Gounod's "Je Veux Vivre" and other arias. Six months later, I was in the Air Force.

I have always loved (almost *needed*) to sing in both the classical and popular idioms, which I did extensively while in the Air Force before ever setting foot in a university. Professional singing financed all my academic degrees, even my Bachelor's. Warned that I would eventually *have* to choose one or the other, I simply continued studying and eventually teaching while continuing to be active—singing opera, oratorio, and contemporary music, and for commercial recording sessions and gigs. My analytical nature plus the exigencies of preserving my voice to cope with the many hours of teaching and singing eventually prompted me to investigate vocal health and hygiene as well as the differences between the various idioms. It was also essential that not a trace of classical vocal influences infiltrate into my pop singing, and vice versa. Hence this book.

To proclaim, as some vocal pedagogues have, that *all* good singing technique is characterized by traditional classical technique and application, and that differences in vocal quality, attack, and phrasing are merely a function of style, is, in my estimation, an oversimplification. While it is true that healthy and expressive vocalism has many elements in common (is resonant, on the breath, is expressive, and communicates), a difference in vocal quality alone implies a specific vocal adjustment and also a difference in proprioception.

Simply stated, singing "Summertime" operatically with orchestra feels and sounds very different from singing "Summertime" as a jazz arrangement with a big band. The first will be in *head voice,* with long legato phrasing, and performed from a written score read by singer and orchestra, while the other will be sung out of the speaking range, with popped articulations (slurs, growls, flips) into notes, liberal phrasing and interpretation, and some improvisation. If the song is performed with a small combo, no music will be written out other than perhaps chord changes, resulting in even more spontaneity and reinvention, with more dynamic range.

Speaking from experience, the proprioceptive sensations differ radically as well. Singing "Summertime" operatically requires breath management in a continuous airflow for effective legato to accommodate the long phrases, smooth attacks, and releases, and must be accompanied by forward focus and head resonance to project over the orchestra, all while largely conforming to the score as written. In singing with a driving big band, however, the notes are popped out, not unlike a jazz trumpet, necessitating much more punctuated staccato attack into words for edge and projection, requiring more flexibility with the breath, shorter, more articulated phrases, and microphone technique that responds more to mouth resonance for projection over the brass. Generally speaking, classical vocalism requires sustained energy over broad phrases, while the manifestation of energy in the jazz/pop idioms comes in spurts, with compressed phrases. Ultimately, for singing to be healthy and project effectively *in both performance idioms and venues,* vocal production must proceed from the breath and away from the throat, must be resonant, and must remain free from extraneous tensions in the body.

More universities are beginning to address the needs of aspiring singers who wish to perform in idioms outside the classical tradition as they pursue careers in the professional music world.

The purpose of this handbook is twofold: To provide some specific, practical suggestions that will prepare the student/vocalist for professional singing opportunities, and to present a pedagogical approach that specifically addresses the vocal needs of singers within the commercial music world, while furnishing insight into healthy vocalism that is idiomatically authentic as well.

The first chapter of the book is directed to the aspiring commercial vocalist and begins with a discussion of the voice as a musical instrument, including the characteristics of a healthy speech pattern and how to maintain it, as well as a specific plan for good vocal hygiene. Chapter 2 serves as a resource for the mechanics of microphone technique, key selection and transposition, lead sheets and songbook preparation, and strategies for developing vocal style and interpretation. Descriptions and prerequisites for performance on a "club date," at a recording session, and for an audition are featured in chapter 3.

Chapter 4 is directed to the voice teacher as well as the aspiring singer and is devoted to developing healthy vocal technique for singing within the commercial idioms. It includes specific vocal exercises for breath management, registration, resonance, articulation, and coordination, as well as stress release and warm-up exercises. Musical theatre pedagogy, including a comprehensive section on "belting," is presented in chapter 5. An annotated bibliography is also included.

The rich variety of vocal styles found within the world of singing serves to illustrate not only the diversity of cultures, but also the myriad ways that human beings throughout the world have devised to communicate their innermost thoughts and feelings. The ever-changing sounds and styles of artistic vocal expression present a formidable challenge for the aspiring professional singer and teacher. It presents a wonderfully rewarding one as well.

ACKNOWLEDGMENTS

In the course of my journeys, both literally and figuratively, I have encountered a number of individuals to whom I owe a great debt of gratitude.

From my *first* school, the U.S. Air Force, I am indebted to CMSgts Dosilee E. Hamilton, Harold Hildebrand, and Raymond Enright for their trust and encouragement while I served as an academic instructor (teaching students who were my age or older!), as well as to Tom Edwards of *Tops in Blue* from whom I gained invaluable "on the gig" experience as an internationally touring musician.

At North Texas State University (now the University of North Texas), I am grateful to my voice teacher, Dr. Pattye Johnstone, whose wisdom I have attempted to impart to *my* students, as well as to Leon Breeden (thanks for the privilege of singing with the 1 o'clock Lab Band!), Jeannine Crader, Grant Williams, David McGuire, and Ed Rainbow for their high standards of musical and academic excellence.

At the University of Miami I owe a very special debt of thanks to Dean William Hipp, as well as to Dr. J. David Boyle, Kenneth Pohlmann, Dr. Lee Kjelson, and the jazz faculty, as well as to my other colleagues in the music school for their inspiration and encouragement through the years. My very deepest thanks go to Professor Lawrence Lapin for his support and encouragement, as well as for his indefatigable dedication and enthusiasm for passing the art and profession of music to new generations of students.

I have learned immeasurably from my dedicated colleagues at the Professional Voice Institute—speech pathologist Vivian T. Harris and Dr. Bruce Weissman—and I am deeply grateful for our association through the years. It's been fun!

Many other teachers and musicians have helped shape my musical growth through the years, including Ray Davidson, Jr., Louis Nunley, Carolyn Stanford, Sheila Marchant Barish, and Deborah Thomas Crawford. I'm also forever indebted to the countless number of musicians I have encountered in my professional gigs and recording sessions through the years who taught me so much by example during my OJT (on-the-job training). I can still recall specific gigs and sessions that were noteworthy in many respects.

Thanks also go to Greta West, Andrea Chaussee Johnson, Michael Johnson, Nuchamon James, and Diane Sutton, all of whom patiently worked with me through the long process of typing and assembling this work.

PART ONE

Preparing to Be a Professional Singer

ONE

Learning about Your Instrument

UNDERSTANDING YOUR VOICE

This section presents a brief overview of the vocal mechanism in order to gain some insight into the operation of your voice. Since our bodies are our instrument, acquiring some understanding of the anatomy and physiology of them can facilitate in acquiring a vocal technique that uses the body most efficiently. For more detailed information, you may wish to consult the number of excellent resources on the anatomy, physiology, and function of the larynx. Some of these are listed in the annotated bibliography in the appendix.

Let us first look at the voice in parallel with other musical instruments. All have an *actuator* or *generator* that sets up a column of air, a *vibrator* (sometimes paired) that serves as a valve converting the air particles into sound waves, and a *resonator*(s) that resounds and reinforces the raw timbre into the unique tone quality of that instrument.

INSTRUMENT	ACTUATOR	VIBRATOR	RESONATOR
Trumpet	Breath	Lips	Bell of the horn
Violin	Bow	String	Sound board
Sax	Breath	Reed	Tubed body
Guitar	Pick/Finger	String	Sound board

For the voice, the actuator is the *breath pressure* produced through exhalation, the vibrators are the *vocal folds,* and the resonators are the *cavities of the throat, nose, mouth, and sinuses.* (The chest cavity is also considered by some to be a resonator; it influences resonance, but is probably not a primary resonator.) The *articulators,* the tongue, jaw, palate, lips, and teeth, convert the basic sound signal into vowels and consonants in order to communicate words and phrases, representing an additional step in sound production for the vocalist.

Insight into the order of sound production is important because it reminds us that the process does not originate with the vibrators, that is, the vocal folds in the throat, but with the breathstream.

Respiration: The Actuation of the Breath Stream

The upper human body is composed of two large cavities, the *thorax,* which encases the lungs, and the *abdomen,* which contains the viscera. Both cavities are separated by the *diaphragm,* a dome-shaped muscle that forms the floor of the thoracic cavity. When we inhale, the diaphragm muscle flattens, creating more room for the inflated lungs in the thorax. Meanwhile, the lower ribs rotate and the abdomen expands, creating a suction so that air does not rush out quickly, but is expelled at a steady rate. Actively maintaining the muscles of inhalation enables us to control exhalation, whether in a steady stream or in pulses, representing breath management for singing.

The Larynx—The Human Voice Box

After the air has been actuated through exhalation, it travels upward, flowing from the lungs through the *trachea* (wind pipe) and through a narrow *glottis,* encountering two "pieces of gristle" (as they have been described by voice scientist Robert Coleman)—two tiny muscles that are similar to little flaps. These flaps are the *vocal cords* (currently referred to as *vocal folds* by speech and voice scientists and henceforward so shall we), which are drawn together (approximated) and begin fluttering in response to the breath, producing phonation.

The primary function of the vocal folds is to serve as a valve to prevent food and fluids from entering the lungs. The trachea, the windpipe leading to the lungs, is directly in front of the esophagus, the food pipe leading to the stomach. When food "goes down the wrong pipe," that is literally what has occurred, and the coughing reflex eliminates the foreign material.

Speech and singing represent a high-order function of the larynx, and research suggests that the larynx was higher in the neck of prehistoric man. The development of speech coincided with the period in which the larynx lowered in the neck to allow for distance between the vocal folds and articulators. It is also higher in the neck for children in order to facilitate the sucking reflex.

The larynx is also considered a secondary sex organ in that it is a way-station for hormonal and glandular changes, as well as nervousness, stress and anxiety. This accounts for the obvious changes during puberty and also during menstruation. The larynx is always in a state of flux, ossifying as we age.

The voice box serves as a rigid structure to permit and ensure an open pathway for breathing. It is composed of one bone, the *hyoid bone,* which forms the top of the larynx. The two major cartilage (soft bone) are the *thyroid cartilage* and the *cricoid cartilage.* The thyroid cartilage, which looks like a breastplate forms part of the Adam's apple. The thyroid cartilage sits on top of the cricoid cartilage, which resembles a signet ring. The vocal folds originate from the center of the breastplate and form a "V" as they attach to the *arytenoid cartilages,* which are two small hammer-like cartilage at the posterior of the larynx.

Extrinsic muscles that support the larynx include a set that raises the larynx (*thyrohyoid*) and a set that depresses the larynx (*sternothyroid*), as well as muscles that depress the hyoid bone and the larynx (*sternohyoid*), and a set that raises and opens the pharynx (*stylopharyngeous*).

In addition to the vocal folds themselves, which are muscle, a set of muscles opens the vocal folds (called *abduction*), while another set closes the arytenoid cartilages and thus the vocal folds (called *adduction*). Another set of muscles at the front of the larynx tense and elongate the vocal folds, while another thickens and relaxes them. There is a set of muscles that rotates the folds as well.

The Vibrators—The Vocal Folds

If you were to take a nickel and draw a "V" on its surface, you would get some idea of the size of the vibrators in the human voice. The vocal folds have elastic properties as well as aerodynamic properties as they respond to the breathstream. They can adjust in length, tension, and thickness relative to the positions of the cartilage and laryngeal muscles, which influence pitch and some aspects of vocal quality.

In *low frequencies,* the vocal folds are relatively short, flaccid, and thick, while for *higher pitches,* the folds tend to be stretched, tense, and thinner. If we revert back to our comparison with other musical instruments, the thicker guitar strings produce the lower tones, while the nylon strings, which also have more tension, produce the higher pitches.

The average male voice tends to be deeper than the female voice due to the comparatively greater length and thickness (15–20 mm for males versus 9–13 mm for females) of the vocal folds as well as the lower vertical placement in the neck. The voices of children tend to be higher pitched due to the relatively short vocal-fold length and higher vertical placement.

We cannot mentally adjust the vocal folds to the precise tension, length in millimeters, and thickness for a target pitch, notwithstanding how that most singers start out by raising and lowering the larynx like an elevator while trying to place pitches. In actuality, the brain sends messages to the muscles and cartilage, revealing how stretched the muscles are, how high the breath pressure is, and the relative position of the cartilage. That is why singing from the throat only gets in the way, and that vocal control stems from breath management and resonance.

The vocal folds are composed of three layers: the *epithelium,* the *lamina propria,* itself composed of three layers, and the *vocal ligament,* the muscle itself. The outer protective layer, the epithelium, is particularly important. It consists of a secreting mucosal covering that is moist, of a slippery viscosity, and that ripples laterally as the vocal folds vibrate. This is referred to as the *mucosal wave* and is very important in protecting the vocal folds as they vibrate, since this outermost layer is the first point of vocal-fold contact. This underscores the importance of staying hydrated, thereby keeping the vocal folds, particularly the mucosa, lubricated. When the vocal folds are dry and swollen, the slippery mucosa does not protect them and the friction can produce thickening or growths such as nodules.

Vocal Fold Vibration

In exploring the organ of voice, one can't avoid a sense of awe at the efficiency and coordination of systems and their intricacy of function within the human body.

Phonation is a by-product of the *elasticity* (length, tension, and thickness) of the vocal folds and *aerodynamic forces* as the vocal folds respond to the breathstream and pressure changes as air flows through the glottis.

In phonation (see figure 1.1), the vibratory cycle begins with *inhalation,* during which the vocal folds open. Just prior to vibration, the brain sends messages to the cartilages and muscles of the larynx, telling the folds to *approximate* (come together). As the breathstream rushes through the narrow glottis, it speeds up and the air pressure along the margins of

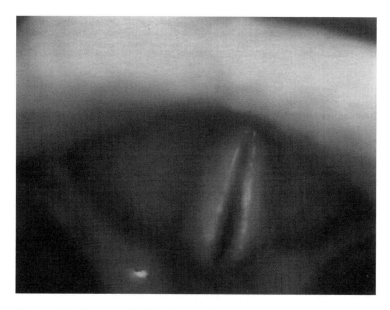

FIGURE 1.1 The vocal folds during phonation.

the vocal folds drops. As a result of this phenomenon, called the *Bernoulli Effect,* the vocal folds are sucked together in adduction for the closed phase of the vibratory cycle.

As air continues to be expelled from the lungs, encountering *glottal resistance* (from the closed vocal folds), pressure builds under the folds, which eventually cannot resist the pressure and blow apart, resulting in the open phase of the vibratory cycle. Hence the vocal folds alternately open and close in a wavelike fashion, from the bottom (lower) portions to the upper (top) portions.

One opening and one closing phase constitutes *one cycle of vibration.* The number of cycles per second (cps) denotes the *frequency* (pitch) of a tone. For example, if a female singer sings A 220, the vocal folds would be relatively flaccid, with little stiffness, so they present less resistance to the breath and flutter more slowly and away from midline. The folds open and close a total of 220 times, hence a frequency of 220 cps. If the vocalist sings A 440, the vocal folds have more tension and therefore present more resistance to the breath. Being stretched, they would be thinner and longer and therefore would not move as far from midline, vibrating faster at a frequency of 440 cps. At 880 cps, the folds would be elongated still further, with very little amplitude.

Registers

As mentioned above, the *thickness, length,* and *tension* of the vocal folds not only affect the frequency of vibration, but also some aspects of timbre as well. As singers gradually ascend the scale, there are certain notes in which the vocalists can discern a subtle but definite physiological adjustment. These perceptual shifts, which correlate with adjustments within the muscles of the larynx are referred to as *registers*.

Experimental studies dealing with registration suggest the existence of at least two distinguishable registers: *chest register* (also referred to as *heavy registration*) and *head register* (also referred to as *light registration*). In addition, in the middle range there are tones that can be differentiated from chest or head register, implying the existence of a *register overlap* or *transitional register.* The *male falsetto* and the *female flageolet voice* (much like a throat whistle) are considered to be registers by some, and are certainly qualities heard within commercial singing styles. However, in these adjustments, only the front one-third of the folds is vibrating at the free edges, which compromises the ability to control dynamics. Extension of the lowest extreme range, called *strohbass* in the male voice, is also regarded as a distinct register by some pedagogues. However, falsetto, flageolet and strohbass, are not considered primary registers.

It is important to emphasize that each set of tiny muscles in the larynx performs a very specific function. A set of muscles opens the vocal folds, and, conversely, sets of muscles close the glottis. There are paired muscles that shorten and relax the folds, while a set of muscles lengthens and exerts longitudinal tension. Finally, there is a set that narrows the glottis as well, serving as an efficiency factor.

In terms of laryngeal adjustments as they correlate to registration, the consensus is that *chest voice* is controlled by the vocalis muscles, and that *head voice* is controlled by the cricothyroid muscles. The cricothyroids are tensor muscles and correlate with pitch. The *shorteners,* the vocalis muscles that are antagonistic to the cricothyroids, also have a tensing component and correlate with loudness within the speaking range as well.

Why is this relevant? If one set of muscles is overworking while the other set of muscles is totally disengaged, the result is straining and eventual vocal deterioration. Allowing muscles to function as they are designed to function and thus achieving muscular balance promotes vocal endurance as well as longevity.

The intrinsic muscles of the larynx can be categorized as:

Closers	inter-arytenoids (oblique and transverse)	brings arytenoid cartilages together and thus the vocal folds together
Openers	posterior crico-arytenoids	tip the arytenoid cartilages back

Tensors	crico-thyroids	stretch and lengthen: high pitches
Relaxers	thyro-arytenoids	shorten and relax: low pitches
Rotators	lateral crico-arythenoids	medial compression: narrow the glottis
Shorteners	vocalis muscles (also stiffen, and act as antagonists to the crico-thyroids)	correlate with intensity

Efficient Vocal Fold Vibration

If you were to consult with an ear, nose, and throat doctor (ENT) because of vocal problems, he/she would examine your vocal folds either with a laryngeal mirror or with video endoscopy or videostroboscopy, in which the folds are viewed using a camera hooked up with fiberoptics. Vocal-fold symmetry, periodicity, amplitude, glottal closure, mucosal wave, and phase difference are examined in order to ascertain if phonation characteristics are optimal. Specifically, the vocal folds are examined for:

Symmetry: Do the folds provide mirror images of each other?
Periodicity: Are the vibratory cycles regular in occurrence?
Amplitude: Is there good movement and extent of horizontal excursion?
Glottal Closure: Are there any gaps? Does the glottis close completely?
Phase Difference: Are there any extremes in the open or closed phase of vibration?

Phonation is also evaluated acoustically to determine the degree of *perturbation,* which is defined as acoustical noise in the voice due to unvoiced sound. *Jitter* describes pitch perturbation; that is, differences in the periodicity or regularity of the glottal waveform. Differences in amplitude or extent of the glottal waveform is called *shimmer.* A high degree of perturbation denotes less-than-optimal vocal-fold condition and efficiency.

Why are all these measures important? The more that phonation displays optimal characteristics of vocal-fold vibration, with low perturbation, the more responsive and healthier your voice will remain over the long term. Singing when the voice is not in "tip-top shape" and thus not a responsive instrument detracts from the pleasure of performing, and it can have a negative long-term effect on a career.

The Resonators

When a vibrator is in tune with the generator, a "resounding" of the sound signal occurs. This is referred to as *resonation* or *resonance.* When the vocal folds are "in tune," that is, coordinated with the breathstream, the

cavities of our body resonate, reinforcing the sound and making it acoustically louder for projection to the listener.

In the human voice, the primary resonators that hold columns of air
and resound the raw timbre emitted from the vocal folds include the *throat*
(*pharynx*), *nose and sinuses* (*naso-pharynx*), and *mouth*. As mentioned
above, singing entails an additional refinement of the raw timbre through
articulation. In voice, the resonators work in tandem with the articulators,
which are the tongue, teeth, lips, palate, and jaw. When a resonator is
united or coupled with an articulator, this alters the size and shape of the
cavities and thus influences tone quality.

For example, the shape and position of the tongue, an articulator, will
influence the mouth as a resonator. The position of the jaw as well as the
palate alters the size and shape of the throat, and thus vocal quality and
resonance. In microphone singing, since the mouth is closest to the head
of the mike, the shape of the mouth and the movement of the tongue, teeth
and lips greatly influence the tone quality within the speaking range.

Acoustically, hard wall and short tubes tend to reinforce high partials
of the acoustical signal, resulting in high pitches and "bright," "edgy" tone
qualities. Conversely, soft walls and long tubes are associated with low
pitches and "dark" vocal qualities. We need only refer to the pipes of an
organ or compare the baritone sax with the tenor or alto saxes to understand these principles.

In singing, if the larynx is high, the jaw is tight and the mouth is
spread, the result will be an *edgy sound*. If the larynx is lower in the neck,
the palate is arched, and the mouth is open freely without jaw tension, the
result is a *rounder, fuller sound*. Notice also that the vowel "o," with the
lips more forward and the mouth cavity elongated, is a darker, deeper
quality than the "e" vowel, with the lips retracted and tight, and the mouth
cavity shortened.

Knowledge of the principles of resonance as applied to the voice is
important in developing reliable vocal technique, because efficiency
involves using the resonators and articulators in the way that they function
most freely and efficiently.

The Articulators

The final phase of tone production consists of the shaping and further
refinement of the breathstream by the articulators, which produce stoppages and/or friction against the air and convert the basic sound-signal
into words. Articulation interacts significantly with resonance because the
shaping of the resonators has already contributed to a large extent to the
acoustical energy and spectrum that define the vowel. The directing of the

vowel forward to the front of the mouth, plus the addition of consonants represents the final step in converting acoustical energy into recognizable words and phrases.

The articulators include the palate, the tongue, the jaw (mandible), the lips, and the teeth. Some pedagogues include the larynx as an articulator due to glottal stops that are found in some languages and categorization of the glottal fricatives [h]. However, it will not be considered at great length in this text.

The *palate* is divided into three distinct parts: the *hard palate,* which forms the roof of the mouth; the *alveolar ridge,* which is the ridge behind the top teeth covered by the gums; and the *soft palate,* which is the soft, muscular structure at the back of the throat from which hangs the *uvula.* The palate can be raised or lowered and interacts with the resonators in shaping the vocal tract for vowels as well as joining with the other articulators, particularly the tongue, in enunciation.

The *tongue* is the most important and active of the articulators, interacting with the resonators and shaping the configuration of the vocal tract. The fact that the tongue is fastened to the hyoid bone, and has contact with the epiglottis, soft palate, and pharynx attests to its importance as a valve and noise generator. The tongue is extremely mobile and flexible (it can move front to back, up and down, can be narrow or lateral, flat or humped), and its edges and body can move independently. There is significant interaction between the tongue and the jaw opening, particularly in the formation of vowels. The tongue is also associated with the pronunciation of diphthongs, as well as in the enunciation of consonants.

The *jaw* or *mandible* is essentially a hinge that is attached to a number of laryngeal and tongue muscles. It is also one of two bones that hold the teeth, and its primary function is chewing. A jaw that is free and allowed to drop or hang, as opposed to being pushed down or kept rigid, facilitates resonance and projection of the tone.

Significant interaction exists between the teeth and jaw. Dental problems, including abnormal jaw development (a jaw that recedes or juts forward) or abnormal tooth development, can have an impact on articulation, resulting in speech problems such as lisp or tongue thrust, as well as contributing to jaw tension. Muscles around the mouth and lips, which may result in lips that are taut or pulled back, can have an impact on articulation as well.

Efficient articulation is represented by loose, supple lips, a free jaw, a flexible and mobile tongue that is free from tension and can move independently, and an elevated soft palate.

The articulators and their various positions include:

1. palate: raised or lowered
2. tongue: front–back; up–down; narrow–lateral; flat–hump
3. jaw (mandible): open–closed; forward–back
4. lips: unrounded–rounded–spread
5. teeth: exposed ("smile")
6. larynx*: glottal stop or fricative

*Some pedagogues include the larynx as an articulator due to glottal stops that are found in some languages and categorization of the glottal fricatives [h]. However, it will not be considered at great length in this text.

The categorization of consonants is as follows:

NAME	HAVING TO DO WITH
1. fricatives	friction
2. plosives or stops	stopping, then exploding
3. labials	lips
4. velars	velum
5. palatals	palate
6. dental	teeth
7. alveolar	gum ridge behind teeth
8. glides or semivowels	vowel-like consonants
9. lingual	tongue
10. voiced or liquid	vibration of folds
11. unvoiced	no vocal-fold vibration

REFINING YOUR SPEAKING VOICE

Is Your Speech Pattern Getting in the Way of Your Singing?

When trumpet players, sax players, guitarists, or keyboard players finish a gig they clean their instruments and pack them away until the next gig or practice session. Not so the vocalist. Unlike instrumentalists, vocalists carry their instrument around with them, using the voice constantly to communicate emotions and ideas. The manner in which singers use their voices every day strongly influences how they sound and what shape the voice is in when it is time to perform.

Singers tend to be verbal individuals, and it is not uncommon for vocalists to employ an abusive speech pattern or pursue a lifestyle that results in vocal fatigue even before they utter a single note in song! At the outset of your career you may have a day job that takes a toll on your voice. Waiting tables is a popular form of employment due to the flexible hours, but projecting the voice over noise makes you a prime candidate for vocal fatigue. Lifestyle adjustments may be required if you like to "party"—socializing in nightclubs and noisy social functions, particularly during a busy performance schedule.

There are some warning signs that suggest your voice is fatigued or showing signs of vocal deterioration. These include:

A breathy or husky vocal quality that tends to be lower in pitch.

Loss of high notes and/or a more pronounced "break" in the voice.

Vocal fatigue and/or hoarseness after a very brief vocal rehearsal or performance.

An audible spillage of air at the start of phonation.

If any of these characteristics are present, consultation with an otolaryngologist may be required in order to view the vocal folds for indications of any swelling or other organic problems. A speech evaluation by a licensed speech pathologist may be a good idea in order to detect any speech habits that contribute to vocal misuse of abuse.

If the voice is generally healthy and responsive, you should nevertheless learn to exercise a speech pattern that maximizes vocal flexibility, range, and endurance. In this section, we will explore elements of speech, examples of vocal misuse and/or abuse, and offer some corrective measures. We will also present a vocal hygiene program, discuss environmental and performance factors that contribute to vocal fatigue, and provide suggestions for relieving symptoms of stress and performance anxiety.

The Parameters of Speech

Ultimately, it is difficult to isolate the components of the speaking voice because of the interrelatedness of all facets of speech. For instance, if you speak with inadequate breath support, you will tend to squeeze from the throat, causing tension in the neck, shoulders, and jaw, resulting in poor resonance and a strident or harsh vocal quality.

For our purposes, we will break down the elements of speech into posture and alignment, breath management, vocal attack, pitch, resonance, loudness, articulation, and tone quality (which can signal inefficiency in the other elements).

Voice disorders are not always associated exclusively with an abusive speech pattern, but may result from the convergence of a number of factors. Let's imagine, for example, that you suffer from a lower- or upper-

respiratory infection, which coincides with an extremely hectic performance schedule that does not permit for vocal rest or pacing. You might also
be experiencing a great deal of turbulence in your personal life, resulting
in considerable physical and emotional stress. The result inevitably
becomes audible. Once a vocal problem has been initiated by a cold, flu,
or other organic problem, less-than-optimal speech habits can allow that
problem to perpetuate or escalate into a vocal disorder that interferes with
singing. Early detection of the danger signs can help mitigate the effects
and underscores the importance of a healthy speech pattern.

What Is a "Normal" or Healthy Voice?

Ideally, a healthy voice is supported with the breath, sounds clear and resonant, is of appropriate pitch and dynamic level, has good rate and fluidity, and appears free from tension.

Posture and Alignment

In speech or singing there should be no impedance of the breathstream as
it travels out of the mouth—no "kinks in the pipe." If you are not aligned,
the result is a strangled, less-fluid tone. In addition, you want to avoid any
stiffness or tight muscles when you perform, particularly as singers are
required to move well and often perform with choreography. The well-
aligned, well-tuned body is essential.

You've probably heard of the imagery of the string at the crown of
your head lifting and straightening your body. You should sense a lengthening of the spine and a feeling of being lifted or elongated rather than
being caved in. Your upper torso should be raised in extension rather than
collapsed into the rib cage. The whole idea is to feel buoyant, with your
shoulders rolled back comfortably and low, rather than slumped and
raised. The appearance of being tall and exuding energy and confidence
are dividends.

The neck should be free-supported by the spine. Many of us tend to
lift the chin and shorten the muscles in the back of our neck, particularly
when being insistent or trying to emphasize a point of view. This has the
effect of misdirecting the airstream, causing it to localize in the throat. In
addition, the jaw, which is a hinge that should drop as it opens, needs to
be pushed down in order to articulate. The chin should be level, and it may
even feel a little tucked-in as a contrast to habitual high positioning or to
compensate for slumped shoulders.

The joints of the body (knees, elbows) should be soft, not rigid or
locked into position. If the knees are rolled back, the result is a swayback,
which breaks body alignment. Rather, the rear end should be tucked in to

keep the knees soft, and your weight should be distributed evenly on the balls of your feet.

If you energize your speech with the breath, it is much easier to maintain posture and alignment. Conversely, if you initiate from the throat or speak too long on one breath, you start to cave in, much like a balloon that collapses from lack of air.

Respiration

Now that you have an unimpeded airway, it should be easier to produce a comfortable inhalation that oxygenates the blood and allows speech to flow out comfortably. There should be relatively little movement in the upper torso (no heaving) when you inhale. If you over-inflate, it is more difficult to control exhalation, as the air tends to be expelled quickly

Audible inspiration represents unnecessary effort and tends to fill your throat with cold, unfiltered, unmoistened air, resulting in a dry throat. *Shoulder breathing* (also referred to as *clavicular breathing*) is inefficient and tends to involve the upper back and neck muscles in speech, resulting in over-exertion and fatigue.

In observing speech pathologists working with voice clients, one of the interesting behaviors they uncover is the tendency to speak to the end of breath capacity—that is, speaking in long phrases without pausing to replenish the breath supply. Speaking to the end of our breath contributes to vocal fatigue. In addition, as the speaker runs out of air, the pitch lowers and there is an unpitched, popping sound that results from the vocal folds vibrating in an open position. This sound is referred to as *vocal fry*. "Frying" constantly can result in vocal disfunction and fatigue. Singers who speak to the end of breath capacity are inclined to transfer this habit to singing as well.

As an antidote to speaking to the end of your breath, read a newspaper or text aloud, replenishing breath support after short phrases. (Breath marks can be denoted by a comma inserted into the text as a reminder to inhale!) Gradually, a rhythm and fluidity of speech will result.

Vocal Attack (Onset of Voice)

The way that you begin a word or sentence—that is, how you initiate tone—can have a strong effect on vocal efficiency as well as tone quality. You don't want to begin a phrase with the throat muscles, but rather allow the vocal folds to be brought together to close the glottis (the space between the vocal folds) in synchronization with the application of breath pressure. This is referred to as *coordinated attack* or *diaphragmatic attack.* (The term *attack,* rather than *onset,* will be used because jazz/pop instrumentalists describe the initiation of a tone as an "attack" into the note [such as a slur, staccato, or tenuto attack] as an aspect of phrasing, and commercial singers parallel such approaches to phrasing.)

Often, singers will initiate a tone by having the vocal folds close first, then apply breath pressure that causes an explosive sound (like a click) as the vocal folds give way. This is called a *glottal attack* (also known as *hard onset, glottal stroke,* and *coup de glotte*). Glottal attacks tend to be self-perpetuating, that is, once one's glottis closes and the walls of the larynx close in, another glottal attack follows as the glottis reflexively reverts to closing again. The result is concentration of muscular effort and tension at the throat level.

At the opposite side of the spectrum, the *breathy attack,* also known as *aspirate attack* or *soft onset,* fails to close the glottis because the vocal folds do not close sufficiently, allowing air to escape. If you lack abdominal strength following surgery or have experienced sudden or extreme weight loss, the result can be a breathy tone. As you strive to compensate for your reduced strength and breath control, you'll have a tendency to localize effort at the throat. Air leakage at the onset of phonation may also signal physiological problems such as vocal-cord swelling or nodules and should be investigated.

As an exercise in eliminating glottal attack, read a paragraph or excerpt from a book or newspaper, placing an "h" in parenthesis before each word or sentence beginning with a vowel. This will make you aware of opportunities for glottalization and help you substitute an imaginary "h" (soft, barely audible) for a glottal attack on initial vowels.

Pitch Level and Voice Range

The pitch level and voice range that you use in habitual speech is significant in terms of vocal efficiency. If the pitch level of your speech pattern is inappropriately low for your vocal mechanism (trying to sound sexy, perhaps?), you will tend to have a throaty vocal quality, often accompanied by a depressed larynx. In addition, you'll tend to initiate tone from the throat rather than with the breathstream. This inclination is also reinforced if the vocal folds are thick due to hoarseness brought on by a cold. Conversely, some individuals use too high a pitch level. The resultant vocal quality tends to be nasal or pinched, like a whine, and the larynx tends to be raised during speech.

As we have seen, *vocal fry* (also referred to as *creaky voice*) can manifest itself at the ends of long phrases, often when the speaker allows the pitch to sag at the ends of sentences. A general pitch level that is too low and fries a lot can result in vocal strain, and in extreme cases can denote a pathological problem such as spasmodic dysphonia.

Do you speak with a monotone? Speech devoid of pitch-modulation or inflection tends to promote fatigue due to the use of a one- or two-note pitch range and correspondingly the same laryngeal adjustment.

Pitch breaks, that is, abrupt shifts in pitch from chest to falsetto, may indicate excessive muscular tension, particularly in the neck and throat. *Phonation breaks,* where the vocal tone is inconsistent and the voice "comes in and out" or "skips," alternating between voice and whispering, may indicate an organic problem as well.

Theoretically, there is a pitch level at which you can achieve the best vocal quality and the desired loudness with the least expenditure of energy, and at which you can initiate the voice with the greatest ease and effectiveness. This pitch level is referred to as *optimum pitch.* While the concept of achieving an ideal pitch level continues to be a matter of debate, it is generally accepted that there exists an optimal pitch range that is most natural and most comfortable for an individual's mechanism. If you are speaking within your optimal range, with good modulation, your speech should feel relatively effortless, with good projection and clarity, and devoid of pitch or phonation breaks or glottal fry.

You should be able to identify your optimal range if you were to say "hm-hmm" softly as if you agree with someone's comment. The tone should be felt in the mask of the face, with minimal vibration in the throat. An alternate way to locate optimal range is to vocalize slowly in a glissando from the highest point in your range to the lowest point. Note the area in the voice that seems to project the loudest as you descend. The vocal range in which the tone swells naturally to its loudest dynamic represents your optimal range.

Pitch perception appears to be influenced by tone placement. For example, speech utterances at a pitch level that maximizes throat resonance will sound lower (and be perceived as lower) than speech that is identical in pitch but focused in the mask.

Resonance

If your voice is resonant, it will be pleasing to the ear and projects naturally. In addition, if the pitch and resonance are optimal (and they interact a great deal), it is easier to articulate and make yourself understood. In order to maximize forward resonance, tone placement should be focused around the mask of the face, with vibration sensed forward in the region around the nose and mouth rather than the throat.

Some people think that if they sense vibration around the nose they will be perceived as nasal. However, *hypernasality* and/or a whiny quality is more often associated with a speech pattern that incorporates significant jaw tension and/or tension in the muscles surrounding the mouth. Assuming that your pitch level is appropriate, hypernasality may be evident if the velum, which closes off the nasal port, is lazy or does not fully elevate to close the nasal passageway.

Hyponasality, or *denasality,* on the other hand, is exhibited when sounds that are normally spoken with nasal resonance are prevented from escaping through the nose. This is often referred to as "the clothespin voice." If you have a head cold, chronic congestion, or severe allergies, you may display hyponasality. If denasality becomes chronic, referral to an ENT or allergist may be indicated.

If you are experiencing consistent problems with hyper- or hyponasality, a visit to the ENT and/or speech pathologist may be in order.

Loudness

If you suspect you are a Type A personality or you are a gregarious individual who enjoys socializing, it is highly probable that you employ *wrong force,* with the accompanying tension in the back of the neck, upper body, and shoulders. This is particularly true as you push while you are attempting to drive home an important point during a discussion. According to some speech scientists, the majority of functional voice disorders is associated with excessive force and use of muscular tension. The result is a weakening of the voice through over-exertion and fatigue.

Less commonly experienced is an inability to project over even moderate levels of background noise, a condition that could denote an organic problem that should receive medical attention.

Be alerted to situations in which you have a tendency to push your voice, such as in "discussions" with family members or in noisy environments. You might also tape yourself while speaking, to determine if you are louder than what is appropriate for a typical situation.

Articulation

The articulators include the jaw, tongue, teeth, lips, and palate. If one overworks to pronounce or if tension exists in the articulators, the result is over-exertion and vocal fatigue.

Watch for tension lodged in the jaw. In extreme cases, if your jaw locks or you have difficulty opening your mouth, you could possibly have a condition known as Temporo-Mandibular-Joint Syndrome (TMJ), in which the temporomandibular joint (near the ears) slides out of its socket, causing a clicking or popping sound. Some students may complain of numbness and headaches as well.

Tongue tension can result in a strangled sound that doesn't project. Conversely, if you have a *lazy tongue,* the jaw tends to become overactive in an effort to compensate. A flexible tongue will enhance clarity and allow you to project your voice with ease.

Tension around the mouth and lips can accompany regional accents such as the "tight-lipped Yankee" or southern accents. Tension also occasionally lodges in the cleft of the chin and may be associated with overall jaw tension. *Malocclusion,* a dental problem related to the bite, can result in rigidity around the mouth and jaw.

The soft palate is the soft structure at the back of the throat, with the velum representing the lower fleshy part from which hangs the uvula. In the elevated or arched position, the soft palate closes the nasal port, which separates the mouth cavity from the nasal cavity. It also directs the sound forward. If the velum is "lazy," the result to a nasal vocal quality. Conversely, if the arch of the palate is exaggerated, the result is a hooty quality.

Clear articulation permits you to project your voice with improved clarity and less effort, resulting in speech that is fluid, unforced, and resonant.

Tone Quality

Your vocal quality is a barometer for how your voice is functioning. For instance, a *breathy voice* suggests that the vocal folds are not coming together sufficiently, resulting in an escape of air. If your voice sounds hoarse, there is a strong probability of rough vocal-fold edges and possible swelling. A honky vocal quality is a husky voice with some nasality. Pushing your voice from the throat can result in a harsh vocal quality, in which the vocal folds are pressed together.

While the above-mentioned vocal qualities reflect the condition of the vocal folds, the following represent qualities related to resonance and articulation. If a voice sounds pinched, there is likely to be some jaw tension with a lowered soft palate. If there is a swallowed quality, the tongue is very likely to be bunched up in the back of the mouth or be depressed. As noted previously, a hooty quality suggests that the soft palate may be over-lifted, while a nasal quality suggests that the soft palate is not elevated enough. A tight, strained vocal sound is normally accompanied by compressed neck muscles and a lifted chin.

Ultimately, the most effective voice is one that is comfortable for you and pleasant to the listener. If people complain that they have difficulty hearing or understanding you when you speak, consultation with a certified speech pathologist might be a good idea. This is particularly relevant for singers, who are not unlikely to become involved in the allied professions of theater or television.

The Music in Language

Every language has a musical ebb and flow, a characteristic that is often tapped into by songwriters in devising melodies to accommodate lyrics. This aspect of spoken language is referred to as *prosody,* which is comprised of the elements of *rate, intonation, stress, fluidity,* and *inflection.*

In listening to someone there is a sense as to whether that individual is excited or bored, based largely on the speed or rhythmic pace of their delivery. This speed or rhythmic pace of delivery is called the *rate of speech.* In music, passages intended to suggest excitement, joy, or agitation are generally brisk. Conversely, passages meant to evoke introspection, intimacy, and hesitation are generally slow. Research suggests there are speech parallels as well. If your rate of speech is too fast, you are probably not pausing often enough to replenish your breath supply. Speech that is too rapid and with few pauses tends to compromise comprehension, since studies have shown that listeners will "tune out" after six or seven seconds of continuous speech.

Intonation refers to variety in pitch level. Effective speech is modulated, as opposed to being monotonous. It explores a variety of pitch levels and inflections, particularly at the ends of utterances. The shape or contour of great melodies often corresponds to the intonation or inflections of the text if it were to be recited aloud like a poem.

Stress represents emphasis, weight, accent, and/or duration as applied to individual words. Rather than the machine-gun type of evenness of words within phrases, there is an ebb and flow within a sentence. Spoken phrases as well as musical phrases gravitate toward important "buzz" words (usually nouns or verbs), which are accorded longer duration or pause. Accessory words such as articles and pronouns are lighter and have less time-value.

Fluidity denotes how language flows. Is it legato and flowing, or does it tend to be choppy? A speech pattern with many glottal attacks will tend to be choppy, as will speech with many ("uh") hesitations.

Vocal inflections are the attacks into words as well as releases. In music, they are represented by slurs, doits, growls, falls, and other ornamentation.

In singing and speaking there is a rhythm and musicality—gravitation to important words and gravitation towards a cadence. It is is probably not a coincidence that many elite singers tend to have a musical speech pattern that they can summon at will.

Elements of Speech

Speech patterns are generally evaluated using the following parameters (use this as an opportunity for self-evaluation):

Respiration (Breath Management): Inhalation and Exhalation

- Do you work too hard when taking a breath, resulting in a lifting of the shoulders?
- Is inhalation audible?
- Do you speak to the end of your breath capacity, or speak in run-on sentences without a breath?

Attack (Vocal Onset): How One Initiates a Sound

- Do you initiate words beginning with a vowel (such as "I" or "and") by using a glottal attack—that is, a clicking sound in your throat?
- Is your tone breathy, with audible escape of air before sound comes out?

Pitch Level (Voice Range)

- Is the voice habitually pitched too high, resulting in vocal strain?
- Is the voice habitually pitched too low, with a great deal of vibration in the throat?
- Are there abrupt pitch breaks?
- Is there evidence of "vocal fry" (an unpitched popping sound resulting from very low pitch)?
- Is speech monotonous or is there good pitch variation?
- Does the pitch drop perceptibly to the point of vocal fry at the ends of sentences?

Vocal Quality (Timbre)

If you were to tape yourself in conversational speech, would you hear some of the following characteristics:

- Throatiness—sound vibrates in the throat as though you had cotton in your throat?
- Breathiness—soft tone; "airy"?
- Huskiness—deep and breathy, as though you have laryngitis?
- Pinched—sounding closed off and nasal?
- Honkiness—sounding husky, but also nasal?

Resonance (Resounding): Where One Senses Vibration

- Is the voice "throaty" sounding as though the voice is lodged in the throat?
- Is the voice nasal (hypernasal) as if the sound is coming out of the nose?
- Is the voice (hyponasal), sounding as though you have a cold?

Loudness (Intensity or Projection)

- Is the voice pushed out or louder than necessary, given the situation or environment?
- Is the voice so soft that you cannot project well enough to be understood?

Articulation (Enunciation)

The articulators are the jaw, tongue, palate, teeth, and lips:

- Do you push consonants out, especially "k" and "p"?
- Are your lips tight when pronouncing certain consonants, especially "r" and "w"?
- Do you have the habit of clearing your throat constantly?
- Do you have a problem pronouncing "s" ?
- Do you have a regional accent?
- Are you afraid to open your mouth? Does your jaw lock or make a clicking sound? Is the jaw tight?
- Have you had extensive orthodontia (braces, etc.)?

Alignment and Tension Areas

Is your upper body rigid, exhibiting the following tension areas?

- Tight shoulders or raised shoulders?
- Compressing or shortening the back of the neck?
- A raised or jutting chin?
- Chin tucked-in excessively?
- Clenched teeth and a tight jaw?
- Locked knees or knees rolled back, resulting in curvature of the spine or sway-back?

MAINTAINING YOUR VOICE

Here are some vocal-hygiene tips that will assist in keeping your voice in good working condition. They are of particular importance when you have got a particularly grueling singing schedule or when you are already under vocal stress due to illness or other physical condition. Do not feel apologetic about being attentive to your vocal condition. All musicians, whether instrumental or vocal, are conscientious about keeping their instrument in tune and good shape.

1. *Keep yourself hydrated by sipping water frequently throughout the day,* especially if you are doing any public speaking, work in a dry environment, or are engaged in long telephone conversations. Drink 6 to 8 glasses of water a day, since water permeates the tissues and helps keep the vocal-tract moist and vocal-folds lubricated.

2. *Drink plenty of liquids* such as fruit juices, which are preferable to carbonated beverages and caffeine. Do steam inhalations (3 to 5 minutes) at least once a day, and increase this to twice or three times a day during periods of vocal stress. Singers have reported being amazed at the differences in singing and speaking as a result of a simple increase in fluid intake.

3. *Monitor your speech.* Avoid strained vocal production when excited during animated discussions. Limit talking when fatigued and avoid communicating from a distance, which encourages yelling or pushing the voice.

4. *Do not compete with ambient noise.* Reduce speech in noisy environments such as nightclubs, street traffic, crowds, etc. Exercise as much self-control as possible at sporting events and rock concerts!

5. *Avoid throat-clearing and excessive coughing.* Throat-clearing is often simply a nervous habit that, like glottal attacks, is self-perpetuating. The urge to clear may be brought on by a tight, closed throat due to nervousness (witness the guest speaker's throat-clearing as he/she mounts the podium). When we "clear," the vocal folds are actually rubbing against each other vigorously, irritating the edges of the folds. Mucus appears at the site of the irritation in order to protect the vocal folds' outer layer, and as we sense the presence of phlegm, we experience the urge to clear again, resulting in a vicious cycle.

6. *Coughing* is especially harmful to the vocal folds as they slap against each other abruptly due to the high velocity of air expelled. *Nodules,* referred to as "cougher's nodules," have been associated with extended bouts of coughing. It is a good idea to reduce speaking and avoid singing when experiencing a cough, since the vocal folds are already thick and irritated.

7. *Avoid whispering or breathy vocal production.* During whispering, air is pushed through the vocal folds, preventing them from coming together and vibrating freely. Eventually, the folds need to be retrained to produce a clear tone.

8. Become aware of common laryngeal irritants such as:

   • *Allergies* you may have acquired to certain foods such as dairy products, molds, foods that are fermented (beer, wine, vinegar, etc.), some grains, and food additives such as monosodium glutamate (MSG), nitrates, or nitrites.

   • *Medications* such as birth-control pills, antihistamines, nasal sprays, hormones, steroids, and "recreational drugs." All of these have been known to affect the vocal tract, and some can be long term or irreversible. Remind your doctors that you are a singer when they prescribe medications so that they can alert you to side effects.

   • *Environmental factors* such as dust, pollen, dehumidified air, stagnant air in aircraft cabins, windy weather conditions, sudden changes in temperature, and dry climates.

   • *Alcohol,* which swells the capillaries and acts as a dehydrant, drying and thickening the vocal folds, and *smoking,* which introduces very hot air directly into the throat and lungs, burning and drying the vocal tract. The combination of smoke and alcohol is particularly damaging due to the drying and thickening of tissues.

- *Fumes and vapors* from strong cleaning agents, aerosol sprays, pesticides, and other inhalants that can result in dry, swollen vocal folds and affect the respiratory system.

9. *Avoid sleep deprivation.* Lack of sleep seriously compromises physical endurance and undermines the immune system, making one less-resilient and more susceptible to illness.

10. *Avoid breathing through the mouth,* particularly in cold air or while sleeping. The nose serves as a natural filtration system that warms, lubricates, and filters the air. If you sleep with your mouth open, try using a cold-air humidifier.

11. *Practice good nutrition* by eating a balanced diet high in protein, complex carbohydrates (pastas and cereals), and fruits and vegetables, and low in fats, oils, and fast foods. Vitamin supplements cannot entirely compensate for the lack of vitamins and bulk fiber that are obtained by eating balanced meals at regular intervals.

12. *Avoid foods that are acidic or that induce gastrointestinal reflux (burping).* Reflux of foods that are high in acid content (such as citrus) can irritate the vocal folds. Avoid eating large meals immediately before retiring for the night.

Medical Problems

Vocal Fold Problems

A diagnosis of *vocal fold nodules* (nodes) is one of the most feared by singers. Nodules (see figure 1.2) are the result of friction or rubbing of the vocal folds against each other due to screaming, shouting, or other forms of vocal abuse as well as poor vocal technique that involves pushing the voice. The condition can be complicated by smoke or alcohol, which results in dryness and thickness, and by allergies.

Nodules start out as the beading of mucus at the eventual site of the nodules, the anterior two-thirds of the vocal folds, which is their vibratory section. Eventually, corn-like growths develop on the edges of the folds that are soft and reddish when newly formed, but can become hard, white, thick, and fibrous if they mature. The symptoms of nodules are hoarseness and fatigue.

Vocal nodules will respond to therapy, but can recur if the abusive practice is not corrected. Usually, vocal rest in combination with voice therapy are recommended. Surgery should be regarded as an extreme measure only after other approaches have proven unsuccessful.

Vocal polyps, which are a growth or protuberance in the membranous portion of the vocal fold, are less defined than nodules but are wider or broader. They can be the result of singing with an upper- or lower-respiratory infection, or as a secondary reaction to a thyroid problem. The symptoms include a constant urge to clear the throat, *diplophonia* (two

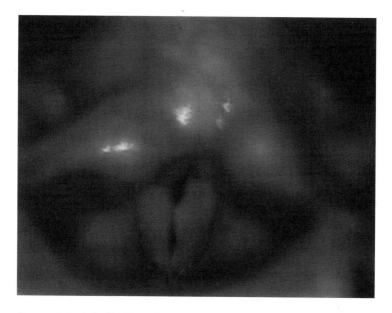

FIGURE 1.2 Spindle-like vibration due to vocal nodules.

audible pitches at once), or sudden voice breaks. Polyps are usually surgically removed, but surgery may be delayed to monitor responses to therapy. Postoperatively, therapy is also recommended.

Laryngitis, whether chronic or acute, can create havoc with a performance schedule and a career if it makes a particularly untimely appearance. In chronic laryngitis, the singer experiences extreme breathiness or a complete loss of voice as a result of vocal abuse, cigarettes, excessive mouth-breathing, or abuse of mouthwashes or alcohol. Symptoms are a low-pitched voice, nonproductive cough, and a throat that aches after brief periods of voice use. The structures are reddened and irregularly thickened, with dilated blood vessels and rounded vocal-fold edges. Brief periods of vocal rest and a vocal-hygiene program are usually recommended for laryngitis.

In *acute laryngitis* the vocal folds move normally, but the symptoms are a sore throat, nonproductive cough, hoarseness, and a mild fever, possibly caused by a viral infection or (less commonly) a bacterial infection. The treatment usually consists of antibiotics, incomplete vocal rest, and a program of vocal hygiene.

If a singer experiences hoarseness, especially in the morning, a bitter taste in the mouth, a lump in the throat, or a constant urge to clear the throat, a condition called *gastroesophageal reflux* may be the cause.

Reflux is the bringing up of acidic, peptic juices that result in swelling and possibly ulcers at the posterior portion of the vocal folds. Antacids and beta-blockers are prescribed, as well as recommendations to alter the sleeping position (head raised), avoid large meals immediately before bedtime, and to avoid acidic foods that tend to irritate.

Endocrine disorders also effect vocal-fold vibration and thus the singing voice. They include conditions such as hypothyroidism, with symptoms of hoarseness, vocal fatigue, and a loss of range. Premenstrual symptoms can also manifest themselves as swelling of the folds due to water retention, vocal fatigue, and loss of endurance, as well as loss of the highest notes in the range and difficulty in maintaining abdominal support.

Singing when the voice is unnaturally hoarse or breathy or during a severe cold or flu can have physiological ramifications over a long period of time. Practicing preventive medicine by following good vocal-hygiene habits and knowing when it is wise to avoid singing (particularly heavy singing) for a period (consult with a doctor when uncertain) can mean that you will rarely, if ever, have to cancel a performance due to vocal problems.

Controlling the Environment and Conditions For Performance

The following performance conditions can contribute significantly to vocal fatigue and abuse:

1. *A poor sound system with no monitors.* Insist on effective monitors (whether "hot spots" or floor monitors) that are positioned close to you and are unobstructed. The most-respected professional vocalists demand two or more monitors as part of their contracts. A qualified sound engineer at the soundboard can verify that the voice is well equalized and projects over the band, while making any necessary adjustments to changing conditions within the performance area.

2. *Poor ventilation and smoke-filled rooms* are characteristic of many performance venues. Staying hydrated and keeping the vocal folds lubricated become essential to maintaining vocal health. Keep water at room temperature on the stage. Some performers even resort to tiny fans to redirect smoke and air from cold vents away from the bandstand.

3. *Loud ambient noise* is another characteristic of certain performance situations. Limit conversation during breaks or move away from the noise. Use hand signals to communicate with band members during performance on stage.

4. *Compromised keys* will take their toll over a four- or five-set evening or extended performances on stage. Having lead sheets available in your key can

persuade accompanying instrumentalists to transpose more cooperatively, and sequencers can be set to change keys automatically.

5. *Poor rehearsal habits* such as singing in full voice over an extended period of time can leave you "fried" for the actual performance. Pace yourself by "marking," that is, singing lightly (not breathy!), substituting for notes in the extreme ranges. Schedule breaks at reasonable intervals, since singing for prolonged periods without them can result in vocal fatigue and hoarseness.

6. *Competing with electric guitars, synthesizers, and sequencers to be heard* is most probably a no-win situation. The human voice cannot compete with electricity! Warped guitar strings and split reeds can be replaced; the vocal folds cannot. Taking time to achieve a reasonable balance between vocalist and instrumentalists during the soundcheck is crucial!

7. *Unrealistic performance schedules* also contribute to vocal deterioration, even under the best conditions. If it is necessary to perform four or five sets a night for six nights a week, pace yourself! If the rigors of travel are a part of your gig, travel with a steamer, maintain good hydration and nutrition, avoid fast food, and avoid sleep-deprivation.

TWO

Preparation for Performance: The Mechanics

"It is a mark of the true professional that he knows how he sounds to others, that he knows how others hear him."

—Henry Pleasants

MICROPHONE TECHNIQUE

It is not an exaggeration to state that the microphone is the commercial singer's best friend. Many singers who possess what could be termed an "average" voice have managed to achieve success through their knowledge of and ability to "work the microphone." They relate to how the microphone "hears" the voice and thus how the audience hears it coming out of the speakers. The microphone can enable you to achieve a warmth, subtlety, and intimacy, since you don't have to worry about projecting in a large performance hall. Knowing how the mike picks up your voice can also help you project over heavy background instrumentation in high-decibel rock tunes.

The initial reaction of most people when hearing themselves on a microphone for the first time is predictable—they are overwhelmed by the amplified sound of their own voice as it reverberates back from the sound speakers. In reflex, the singer or speaker typically pulls away from the mike, effectively negating the benefits of having it. After observing many an impromptu public speaker who was told to "speak up" due to "microphobia," this phenomenon appears to be a somewhat universal trait.

In order to be an effective and healthy professional singer you should regard the microphone as a valuable ally, for it enables you to project the vocal sound with less exertion while achieving a relaxed, conversational approach that would not be possible acoustically, particularly in large performance settings. You should luxuriate in the sound as it is fed back to you from the monitors or house speakers, much like the electric guitarist relates to the sounds that proceed from the guitar amp. The vocalist's instrument is the voice as amplified by the sound system, magnifying flaws as well as enhancing the acoustical characteristics of the individual voice, transforming it into a totally new instrument.

The Microphone

The microphone is a *transducer*, converting acoustical energy to electrical energy. The primary purpose of the microphone is to convey the vocal sound to a sound system, where it is amplified and again converted to acoustical energy at the loudspeaker. When sound systems and the microphone initially appeared on the scene, vocalists were liberated from the necessity of projecting just to be heard. Some reverted to "crooning," in which the vocalist assumed an intimate, light, conversational style. However, in an instance of having come full circle, the emergence of electronic instruments as backup, from the electric guitars for rhythm & blues and rock & roll in the 1950s to the synthesizers, sequencers, and drum machines of the 80s, plus the "hard," intense styles of contemporary music, reintroduced the necessity for projecting the voice. Thus, knowing how to work the microphone can enable you to be warm and subtle on a sensitive ballad, while projecting intensity and strength for the hard rocker. Knowing how the microphone "hears" the voice can also help you project without pushing, thus preserving the instrument.

A professional commercial singer should own his/her own microphone, mike cable, and transformer, display an awareness of the directional response, working distance and impedance of the particular microphone in use. Appreciation for the distinguishing characteristics of the various microphones available in the marketplace and knowing what to look for in purchasing a microphone is essential. The commercial vocalist must be able to orient himself/herself to the vocal sound as it proceeds from the monitors or house speakers, know how to test the mike for maximum effectiveness, and be able to avoid "popping" and other undesirable extramusical sounds. Finally, singers should have some knowledge of how sound systems work, and be aware of factors influencing sound reinforcement and equalization of the voice.

Directional Response

Microphones can be classified according to the following directional responses:

1. *Omnidirectional* or *undirectional*—a microphone that receives sound from all directions.
2. *Unidirectional*—are most sensitive to sound originating from one direction only, usually directly in front.
3. *Bidirectional*—sensitive to sounds from the front and rear; also referred to as a figure-eight because of the response pattern.
4. *Cardioid*—derives its name from its heart-shaped response pattern, accepting sounds from the front and sides, while suppressing sounds from the rear.
5. *Supercardioid*—employs a tight heart-shaped response pattern, making it especially efficient with monitors.

As a general rule, the tighter the response pattern, the more pivotal the directional response. Recording engineers may classify microphones by their design, referring to them as

1. *Dynamic*—have moving coils.
2. *Velocity* (pressure gradient)—use a ribbon.
3. *Condenser*—use charged plates.

Condenser mikes, which are powered by batteries or a "phantom power" supply, are delicate and relatively expensive. They have been known to lose calibration after only a few instances of having been dropped accidentally. The condenser mike is therefore more frequently found in the recording studio, while the more-durable dynamic microphone is more practical for live performance. Of importance to singers is the fact that a *dynamic mike* with a *cardioid response pattern* is considered to be more flexible, dependable, and adaptable to performance situations, whether indoors or outdoors.

For vocalists, the following companies offer comparably priced microphones that have demonstrated reliability and durability for most performance situations: Audio-Technica AT 814; Beyer Dynamic M 500; Electro-Voice PL 80, PL 91A (with on/off switch, & PL95); and Shure SM 58 and Shure Beta.

Low or High Impedance

Impedance refers to the opposition of a component such as a microphone to the flow of electrical current. This electrical specification is used to note microphones as being either of *high* or *low impedance.* Most professional-quality mikes are low impedance. While high-impedance mikes are not necessarily inferior, the low-impedance mike permits the use of cable over a long distance without compromising high-frequency response. There is less probability of undesirable hum or feedback. If one has a low-impedance mike and the amplifier requires high-impedance input, one can purchase a line-matching transformer, such as the Shure A 95P or the Electro-Voice Model 502 CP, which makes the microphone adaptable to any kind of sound system.

Microphone cable, that is, the wire connecting the microphone with the amplifier, is also very important to the quality of sound. The average length of mike cable is 20 feet, which is a practical length for the majority of performing situations. Care must be exercised when moving heavy equipment over cables, since compressing the wire within the cable might compromise cable integrity. The connectors on either end are particularly vulnerable to damage.

Working Distance

Conversations with professional sound engineers for renowned artists reveal that some vocalists stay "right on top" of the mike, lips almost touching the microphone's grill. Other singers maintain a considerable distance from the mike. Ultimately, the *working distance* from a microphone is dependent upon the particular microphone in use, the sound system, and the sound engineer's personal working style. The characteristics of the performance venue factor in as well.

Although working distance varies, in general the microphone should be positioned no further than six inches away from the mouth. Very subtle shifts in direction or distance can affect the timbre of the singer's voice as well as the feeling of "presence," so it is important to "work" the mike, remaining alert to the way it "hears" your own individual instrument.

The vocalist must remain ever-cognizant of distance when pulling back from the microphone for notes that are radically higher or louder so as not to overload the mike or sound system and thus create distortion. The degree to which the mike can be pulled away depends on its sensitivity. Some mikes have a sensitivity that attenuates quickly (just a matter of inches), while others do so more gradually. Some vocalists effectively avoid distortion or "popping" by singing slightly "over the microphone" or slightly to the side when singing peak notes or passages. But they must be careful to revert back to the general working distance after they have adjusted for these passages. With the exception of climactic points, the singer must maintain a consistent positioning in relation to the mike.

Failure to do so severely compromises the engineer's ability to achieve consistent sound quality and dynamics.

Popping and Windscreens

While maintaining a close distance to the microphone is important, there is the increased likelihood of "popping," "smacking," or other distracting, extraneous sounds. In order to limit such undesirable effects, one should sing slightly over the microphone or at an angle to it. In this way, sibilant sounds such as "p," "b," and "s" will not be distorted nor create percussive sounds.

Windscreens are very useful in eliminating extraneous sounds or when performing outdoors where windy conditions can become a factor. Also referred to as "windshields," "pop filters," or "socks," windscreens are effective in preventing moisture from building upon the microphone head. In instances where sibilants such as the "s," "ch," and "t" are distorted, reduction of these explosive bursts of air can alleviate the problem to some degree without compromising intelligibility. Because of its ability to reduce sibilant noise and protect the microphone from moisture damage, the windscreen should be considered to be mandatory equipment.

Proximity Effect

While it is desirable to stay on top of the mike, it must be noted that with cardioid and bidirectional microphones a "boomy" vocal quality can result when positioning the mouth too closely to the mike. Excess air spillage or excessively breathy sounds cast directly onto the mike can also result in considerable distortion. This phenomenon is a result of *proximity effect,* which describes an audible increase in bass response as the mike is moved closer to the sound source. Male singers (who already possess the low frequencies) may use proximity to further boost the low end. Female vocalists may prefer to add lows to the vocal timbre in order to make the sound richer and fuller, with a wide spectrum of harmonics. In addition, according to Clifford (1982):

> The increased bass energy produces a high signal to ambient noise ratio. This furnishes the vocalist with greater isolation from the accompanying instrument, supplying greater vocal penetration to rock groups and lessened acoustic feedback in some applications. Sometimes proximity effect appeals to vocal performers because it lets them "shade" their voices. But this same bass emphasis under other conditions could lead to "muddy" recording and/or sound transmission.

Whenever the proximity effect is used, it is crucial to maintaining a consistent distance between mouth and mike, otherwise the timbre of the voice can vary radically. Despite the proximity limitations of directional mikes, the bleed from outside sources is appreciably reduced and can help to isolate the voice from the wall of sound represented by electronic instrumental accompaniment.

Equalization of the Voice

Equalization of the voice is defined as a modification or adjustment of the frequency response of a sound system. In general, frequency is normally broken down into what is referred to as *bass* (lows), *midrange* (mids), and *treble* (highs), corresponding to the areas of the sound spectrum. These frequency bands can be boosted or attenuated depending upon the vocal quality sought. Frequency adjustments depend on room acoustics, the microphone characteristics, and the vocalist's inherent vocal quality.

For example, if a voice tends to sound "boomy," it would be counter-productive to boost the low frequencies and ignore the high-frequency adjustments. Conversely, a female vocalist with a high, focused vocal quality may wish to boost some low in order to add fullness and depth to the vocal timbre.

It is useful to experiment with the response of various microphones. For instance, if you hold the mike at a great distance, the high partials of the voice are emphasized, resulting in a metallic quality and a loss of presence. If you sing directly into the mike, one will notice that the entire tonal spectrum (low, mids, and highs) is enhanced, the tone quality is "present," and you can convey a sense of "immediacy"—the sense of being "right there." Every nuance is reinforced and becomes audible. It is a much simpler task for the sound engineer to enhance the vocal sound if the vocalist maintains predictable microphone positioning. If the singer is inconsistent, the sound engineer is relegated to controlling intensity at low levels in order to prevent sudden bursts of sound that result in distortion. If there is no engineer, you can better insure that you are "present" in the mix.

Perhaps the best way to acclimate yourself to the microphone is to experiment with a variety of mikes, thereby determining their individual response characteristics. The more experience you have singing with the microphone, the easier it will be to relate to and become comfortable with amplified sound. Becoming sensitized to the reinforced vocal sound as it proceeds from the sound speakers is of paramount importance. In commercial singing, the voice as instrument is the sound *as it is picked up by the microphone.* This distinction is crucial to becoming a commercial vocalist with good microphone technique.

Sound Reinforcement

In performing situations in which the vocalist has some control over the sound, it is useful to understand aspects of *sound reinforcement*. Sound-system controls may include a *graphic equalizer* to adjust frequency response, as well as *reverb* and *volume controls*. In addition, each *console channel input* has individual controls affecting lows, highs, and on most amplifiers, mid-range response as well. It is important to adjust the system controls in accordance with the acoustical properties of the performance setting for an overall effect. Individual console-channel controls can then be used for the specific needs of the vocalist or instrumentalist being amplified on that channel.

Once system controls have been set, the levels of the individual channels should be set at a nominal level, starting out with a "flat" sound and making adjustments very gradually and conservatively. Extreme adjustments can result in over-compensation and a loss of fullness or naturalness. In addition, feedback in the form of a high squeal or low hum can result. The high, shrill feedback usually indicates that the "highs" are boosted to an extreme; a low-pitched hum may denote that lows are boosted excessively. Maintaining frequency adjustments at a conservative or "safe" limit permits boosting of the overall levels on the master, resulting in a full sound with more "presence" but without feedback.

Before adding *reverberation* ("reverb") or echo, it is important to take the acoustical properties of the performance setting into consideration. For instance, if the room or hall can be characterized as having a lot of hard surfaces (marble walls and plaster ceilings, for example), sounds tend to "bounce off" and resound, resulting in reverberated "live"-sound characteristics. Conversely, if the surfaces are heavily carpeted or draped, the sound will tend to be "dry," with little reverberation. Hence, reverb controls may need to be boosted. It is important to remember that the addition of effects such as reverb or digital delay can affect intelligibility and clarity, as well as vocal quality.

Good equalization is generally more satisfactory than boosting vocal frequencies to make them heard above the instrumentals, which can result in feedback problems. Of particular relevance to singers is the phenomenon of *midlift*, in which a particular narrow range of frequencies is selectively amplified without reducing the remainder of the sound (Nesbitt 1983). Enhancing the formant frequencies and resonance qualities of a voice or instrument give each instrument its character. It enables the voice or instrument to emerge as a distinctive timbre within much of contemporary music's "loud and densely structured sound" (Nesbitt 1983). Midlift contributes significantly to volume by adding "presence"—that quality that allows the voice to be brought forward perceptibly, making the subtle shadings of vocal quality travel directly to each individual listener's "lap." "Presence" as achieved through midlift contributes to a feeling of being directly beside the performer, even in an enormous performance venue.

Thus, it is advantageous to take the time to equalize the voice effectively in order to:

1. allow it to assert itself as a distinguishable timbre within the performance ensemble;
2. attenuate intruding instrumental levels; and
3. leave the vocal sound "clean" and enhance communication and clarity of text.

Monitors

One of the most difficult adjustments microphone singers must make is to relate to the sound *as it proceeds from the house speakers or stage monitors.* This is essential because the sound emanating from the sound system is what the audience is hearing—not what is emerging directly out of the mouth. It is important to have monitors and a monitor mix that accurately reflect what the microphone is "hearing" and transmitting and thus what the house is hearing.

Amplification reinforces certain vocal characteristics and attenuates others. It also enables one to achieve presence, subtlety, and intimacy. There are certain harmonics and breath-pressure adjustments that are audible on microphones but that are lost completely when singing acoustically. This is particularly apparent in the case of the female vocalist, who is able to achieve fullness and richness of vocal quality when lower-frequency components become more perceptible on the microphone. Just as the electric guitarist must relate to the sound as it proceeds from the amplifier, so must the vocalist relate to the vocal sound as it is transformed by the mike. The ability to monitor oneself is crucial to artistic and intimate communication on the microphone. It also represents a key factor in vocal health and longevity as well.

When singing in larger "houses" or with heavy instrumental backup, the stage monitors serve two vital functions for the singer:

1. they enable you to hear yourself as the audience hears you; and
2. they protect you by enabling you to counteract the tendency to push when you are unable to hear yourself.

The latter phenomenon is referred to as the *Lombard effect* and is recognized in the world of speech pathology. The Lombard effect states that you will tend to push or speak loudly as reflex when you cannot hear yourself. This effect is in action when someone automatically speaks very loudly while wearing earphones. This example is usually quite comical, since the speaker wearing the earphones seems totally unaware of how loudly he/she is speaking. However, the ramifications of such forcing due to the absence of a good monitoring system are serious for the singer, since it contributes significantly to vocal abuse and misuse.

Sophisticated monitoring devices are constantly emerging that make it easy to hear oneself distinctly above the band and others on stage. These include tiny monitors that are no larger than the size of hearing aids or ear plugs that can be planted inside the ear. Performers who have had the opportunity to use them maintain that the degree of isolation and quality of sound derived from these tiny monitors is first-rate, rivaling that achieved in the recording studio. As is true of new technological advances, the cost of such state-of-the-art monitoring devices should eventually decrease, making them more accessible to the average performer.

It is interesting to note that the contractual terms of the majority of distinguished professional vocalists include strict provisions for an effective monitoring system. Otherwise, these artists reserve the right of refusal to perform, underscoring their understanding of the importance of good monitors.

Head Mikes

Head mikes are becoming more prevalent in live performances, whether by major touring artists whose act involves a great deal of dancing and movement or by touring Broadway shows. Head microphones are so delicate that in the case of Broadway musicals, the sound technician is the only person authorized to wire the microphone (which is usually covered by a wig worn by the actor) in place. Conversations with performers who have played major roles in such shows as *Phantom of the Opera, Les Misérables,* and *City of Angels* reveal that the vocalists sing as though they were performing acoustically rather than "playing the microphone." The position of the microphone around the hairline emphasizes forehead and head resonance, facilitating vocal projection over a mix of prerecorded as well as live instrumental accompaniment.

On the other hand, in the case of rock & roll artists, the microphone is similar to that used by a switchboard operator, being close to the singer's mouth. Thus it amplifies sound as it proceeds out of the mouth in the same manner as its hand-held counterpart. The singer cannot "play the mike" and adjust for notes that are out of balance, so vocal technique and dynamic control in combination with a sound engineer who is very familiar with the artist's mike technique and style all become crucial. Head mikes and wireless microphones may leave the singer at a loss as to what to do with the free hand (since there is no mike cable to play with), but they do serve to free-up the performer for choreography and movement over a larger performing area.

Vocal Technique on the Microphone

It is important to consider the following necessary adjustments when singing with a microphone versus singing acoustically:

1. *Inaudible inhalation*—since the mike picks up even the most subtle adjustments in breath pressure, inhalation must be accomplished with an open throat (beginning of a yawn) so that it is inaudible. In addition to being a distraction, audible inhalation reflects shallow air intake, with cold, dehumidified air contributing to the drying of the throat. It should be avoided in acoustical singing as well.

2. *Overblowing*—a concentrated breathstream directly onto the head of the microphone can result in distortion. It is for this reason that the pure vowels so important for projection in acoustical singing can become a problem on the microphone. This is especially true of the "u" vowel. Awareness of proximity is crucial so that you can sing over the mike, thereby avoiding distortion.

3. *Mouth resonance*—on the other hand, mouth resonance becomes very important in terms of projection as well as timbre in rock & roll and other high-energy styles that require projection over electronics. The mike is particularly sensitive to air that proceeds out of the mouth; therefore the shape of the mouth and coupling with the tongue greatly enhance projection and influences timbre. To experiment, sing the "o" vowel on the microphone, rounding the lips gradually from "a" to "o." At some point you will sense and hear the air as it travels forward and the tone becomes significantly louder. (Be sure you are not pulling the jaw back or that tension exists around the mouth.)

4. *Dynamic control*—the sensitivity of the microphone to subtle changes in breath pressure will expose lack of dynamic control. Although engineers can compensate for lack of consistency (along with compressors and other electronic gadgets) within the studio, that luxury is not always available in live performance. Interestingly, less-experienced vocalists can have difficulty maintaining a medium dynamic level clearly and consistently. Singers who can sing only very softly or very loudly sacrifice vocal presence, because they have to "play the mike" constantly to compensate for sudden bursts of sound. This underscores the importance of practicing on the microphone whenever possible. The degree of effort vis-à-vis intensity is vastly different on the microphone than it is acoustically. If one has been singing a great deal on the microphone, the vocal effort associated with projection when making the transition to acoustical idioms can be surprising as we are reminded of how much the mike actually assists in tone projection.

5. *Enunciation*—lingering on voiced consonants (l, d, b, m, n, z, g, r, v, j) (which have also been referred to as "liquid consonants" because they continue voic-

ing) keeps the sound forward and contributes to warmth and sensitivity in interpretation. It also enhances intelligibility and presence. Tension around the mouth and lips results in popping as well as a loss of clarity. Tongue flexibility is important for clarity, especially in soft, subtle passages.

6. *Key selection*—comparatively speaking, female vocalists can perform in lower keys on the microphone than when singing acoustically. While head resonance facilitates "ring" and projection in acoustical mediums, the microphone tends to focus sounds as well as distort at very high frequencies, contributing to harshness. (In the studio, the engineer will often resort to using a "limiter" or compressor in order to cut-off high partial energy and thus avoid distortion.) While the lower range of some female voices may not project acoustically at low intensities, the microphone can pick up and enrich the relaxed speaking range, allowing more conversational approaches and intimacy in certain passages.

Common Misapplications of Microphone Technique

1. *Not taking sufficient time to test the microphone.* Take time to test the microphone, because once in the middle of a performance you really do not have the luxury to make adjustments. If the volume levels are too soft, you lose the ability to communicate subtle nuances and shadings; over-singing is often the result as you try to compensate for lack of projection.

2. *Not taking sufficient time to equalize the voice.* Take responsibility for the quality of your voice over the microphone. Nothing is more defeating then to have to contend with sound that is muddy (and people complain because they can't understand the words) or sound that makes your voice sounds "tinny" without any fullness or depth.

3. *Not providing the sound engineer with sufficient information regarding specific reinforcement needs and aspects of your individual vocal quality and projection.* The sound check allows the engineer to set levels, so be certain that your sound check goes through the gamut of ranges and styles. You might also like to point out those tunes in which you might like effects (reverb, delay, etc.). If you do not have an engineer, then you must know how to adjust the system for *your* voice, rather than putting yourself at the mercy of others. After all, you know your voice best.

4. *Not verifying that the monitor mix corresponds to the house mix.* Many a singer has held back because the monitors were loud, resulting in a lack of projection in the house. While it is important to hear yourself clearly, the monitor mix should be close to the house mix.

5. *Not relating to the sound as it proceeds from the sound speakers and/or monitors.* You will be unable to monitor yourself if you relate only to what is coming out of your mouth. Instances of distortion and feedback will also go unnoticed.

6. *Positioning yourself too far from the mike.* Get comfortable with the sound of your voice as it comes back to you from the speakers. Don't let the volume of

sound intimidate you. The farther away you are from the mouth, the more metallic the sound.

7. *Positioning yourself too close to the mike, resulting in distortion.* Be aware of the proximity effect when singing right into the grill, which can result in a "muddy" quality in some voices. Aspirate sounds with the excess airflow can also produce distortion.

8. *Not pulling away from climactic notes or passages.* The result is distortion and harshness, undermining the impact of the climax and disturbing the listener.

9. *Pulling back excessively at climactic points.* Some singers pull back so far on their big notes that they undermine the buildup to the climax. Your adjustments should be gradual and subtle.

10. *Not singing at an angle, over the top of the mike, or to the side to prevent popping.* Use a windscreen if popping is a problem. Microphones that are noisy when held will probably tend to pop more than less-sensitive mikes.

Purchasing a Microphone

It is wise for the pop/jazz vocalist to invest in a good microphone as soon as possible. If a sound system is not readily available or is too cumbersome, purchasing a portable amplifier can provide the opportunity for the student singer to experiment with microphone technique. Relatively small electric bass amps are particularly suitable for this purpose since they are portable. Amps should be able to be adjusted for low-, mid-, and high-frequency equalization, and have a reverb unit.

Each individual vocalist possesses a truly unique instrument, with distinct characteristics and acoustical properties. Therefore, while one microphone may be ideal for a certain individual, it may be totally unsuitable for another. When shopping for a microphone, you should try to insure that the amp and equalizer remain constant while testing each microphone in order to more-accurately compare the responses. Then evaluate these items:

1. Does the voice sound full and warm, or is the tone too thin?
2. Does the microphone convey the lower part of the range? Does it convey the high register?
3. Is it sensitive, or must one sing loud before it responds?
4. Is it adaptable and durable for use in a variety of performance situations?
5. Does it seem to distort too readily when you get close or moderately loud?
6. Is the vocal quality shrill or muddy?
7. Does the microphone have an on/off switch? If not, does the mike cable?
8. Is it low or high impedance?
9. Is it overly sensitive to handling, producing hand-noise?

10. Does it enhance your vocal quality?
11. Does the particular model under consideration have a good performance record?
12. Does it respond well to a variety of vocal sounds and dynamics during the test?

Remember! Know your microphone and sound system as well as an electric guitarist knows his/her amplifier and effects. Both are crucial to the instrument's overall sound and its impact on the listener.

KEY SELECTION: CHOOSING THE IDEAL KEY FOR A SONG

What Is the Ideal Key?

Most experienced singers are inclined to perform a song in:

1. the key in which the song was recorded by the original artist;
2. the key used in the published version; or
3. the key in the band's repertoire.

All of these approaches in choosing a key do not take into account that the published or recorded key may not be the ideal one for *your* voice. Why perform a song in someone's else's key? Each human voice is a totally unique instrument characterized by differing vocal qualities and intensity levels in different ranges. If a song is keyed too high, you may have to strain throughout; conversely, if the key is too low, you may have difficulty projecting. Therefore the key in which you choose to perform a song can strongly affect the impact of your vocal performance.

The optimal key for singing, like the optimal speaking range, enables you to achieve with ease the desired vocal quality and control of intensity. You can avoid the tendency to push throughout your vocal range. A comfortable key makes it easier for you to build up to a climax on a ballad, because you can begin the song with a soft, warm, intimate approach that builds naturally as you increase intensity and breath support for louder passages. Worrying throughout a tune whether you are going to be able to make that big, climactic high-note can compromise your communication during the rest of the song. Why hinder yourself unnecessarily?

The optimal key choice should also make it easier for you to enunciate, making the ever-important song-text intelligible to the listener. In classical singing, song passages that tap into the higher notes in one's vocal range necessitate increased vowel modification in order to avoid vocal constriction. Within the context of a pop tune, such vowel modification results in distorted text that does not sound natural, "real," or conversational. The female vocalist, particularly, will not be using the soprano head voice but be singing out of the speaking range, so it is especially crucial that the key choice coincides with the optimal speaking range.

To some degree, this acoustical fact is acknowledged within the classical repertoire by voice categorization (soprano, alto, tenor, and bass), along with the subdivisions within these vocal categories (coloratura, lyric, spinto or dramatic soprano), for example. The criteria used as a basis for such categorization include the vocal "color" and richness of voice quality as well as the range in which the voice projects and asserts itself acoustically over a large orchestra or performance hall. Many a classical singer has suffered an abbreviated career due to performing repertoire that was not suited to the size and range of his/her voice. *Key choice and vocal range within the commercial idioms are also crucial to enabling the voice to project as a distinguishable timbre over electronic instruments and other loud accompaniment.*

Failure to choose congenial keys for the bulk of your repertoire can result in a gradual limitation of loudness levels and a loss of dynamic contrast. Over a period of time, the exertion required to deal with uncomfortable keys results in vocal fatigue and an inability to pace oneself during strenuous performance schedules. Therefore, key selection has ramifications for vocal health and longevity.

Identifying the Ideal Key for a Song

Here are some steps toward finding the optimal key for a song that best displays your instrument:

1. Sing through the entire song away from the piano so that you are not influenced by the key in the written music. Go through the entire song, because many songs modulate to a higher key at the bridge. Sing "on microphone" whenever possible, because sounds that project adequately on the mike may sound acoustically too low and too soft.

2. Only after finding a comfortable key, do you proceed to the piano to find out what key you've been singing in. Remember, not every tune starts on "do," the tonic note of the key. For example, the song "Somewhere" from *West Side Story* starts on "sol" or on the 5th of the key.

3. Next, experiment with adjacent keys ($1/2$ step up or $1/2$ step down), keeping in mind that the climax of the song usually represents the highest and most powerful notes. Worrying about whether you will be able to hit that big high-note at the end of the song can distract you and interfere with communication

throughout the body of the tune. The climax of the song should lie within a vocal range that is comfortable, even when you may be having an off-day and your voice is not at its best.

4. Avoid sharp keys—key signatures with too many sharps (E major, F# major, G# minor, and other keys with more than two sharps). Sharp keys place the trumpets and horns in awkward keys, since they are transposing instruments. Rather than performing in the key of B (5 sharps), choose the key of B$^\flat$ or C in order to accommodate the instrumentalists. Most standard tunes are originally in flat keys.

5. Bear in mind that lowering or raising the key a semitone could result in a subtle but definite alteration of the vocal quality and vocal color. If the song lies in the lower part of your range, the sound may be warm and sultry or result in a dark quality that fails to project well over the instruments. Conversely, if the song lies in the upper part of your range, the result could be an edgy, bright quality that projects well but borders on harshness. This phenomenon should be taken into account when experimenting with key choice.

6. Select a key that enables you to sing under the most stressful conditions rather than saddling yourself unnecessarily with a key that requires you to be in optimal vocal and physical shape. Occasionally, one is relegated to singing under less-than-ideal physical and musical conditions. The choice of a comfortable key can help alleviate some of the pressure inherent in such situations.

7. When transposing, the chord letter will change, but the extension will remain the same. For example, transposing up the interval of a perfect 5th from C^7, the chord would become G^7.

8. Table for transposition:

To transpose	a major 2nd	two $^1/_2$ steps on piano
	a minor 3rd	three $^1/_2$ steps
	a major 3rd	four $^1/_2$ steps
	a perfect 4th	five $^1/_2$ steps
	a perfect 5th	seven $^1/_2$ steps

9. Here are some indicators that suggest you have identified the optimal key for a particular song selection:

   • you can display a wide range of dynamic levels (not just loud, louder, loudest!) and can control dynamics effectively
   • you are easily understood, and it is easy to enunciate when communicating the text
   • you don't have to "work hard" throughout the entire tune. You are in control!

10. Remember! Judicious key selection enhances vocal projection, allows for dynamic contrast, and enables you to pace yourself during a gig, helping you to stay healthy and keep performing.

Hand Signals for Calling Keys

In order to identify key changes during a song medley, a system of hand signals has been devised. Rather than call out the new tune and the new key, the leader signals the key, the rhythm section modulates to the new key and vamps until the entrance by the vocalist or instrumentalist. The hand signals are as follows:

KEY	SIGNAL
Key of C	Thumb and index finger rounded to C shape (no sharps or flats)
Key of F	Index finger pointing upward (like a number 1) for one flat
Key of B$\flat$	Two fingers (index and forefinger) pointing upward for two flats
Key of E$\flat$	Thumb and index finger in a circle; remaining 3 fingers upward for 3 flats
Key of A$\flat$	Four fingers up for 4 flats
Key of D$\flat$	Entire hand for five flats (not a common key)
Key of G	Index finger pointing downward for one sharp
Key of D	Index finger and forefinger pointing downward for 2 sharps
Key of A	Three fingers pointing downward for 3 sharps (thumb and index finger in a circle)
Key of E	Four fingers pointing downward for 4 sharps. The key of E is a good key for rock & roll, and is one favored by guitarists because of the open strings

In general, it is wise to avoid sharp keys beyond the key of A, because it places the saxes and horns, the transposing instruments, in awkward keys (F# and B, respectively). It is obviously also important to know key signatures so that you can relay your key correctly. Remember, in most situations flat keys are up and sharps are down, contradictory as that may seem.

LEAD SHEETS AND SONGBOOKS

Lead Sheets

The more a vocalist is aware of the chord changes of a tune as well as what is going on in the rhythm section, the more control she/he can exert over the performance situation. Therefore, in addition to the ability to transpose (which is discussed in the above section, Key Selection), a singer should be able to write what is referred to as a *lead sheet* or *chord sheet* for a song, particularly if the song is obscure or complicated. What follows is a minicourse on writing a simple lead sheet.

A Lead Sheet consists of:

1. the melody and chord changes with their extensions
2. the song lyrics
3. song form (A-A-B-A-, etc.)

In preparing your first lead sheet, it might be helpful to purchase a published song sheet as a model. Your lead sheet will have the same form as the published version, with repeat signs, bridges, etc., but will consist only of the melody, chords, and song lyrics.

Writing out notes is not necessary, although as you become experienced, you may want to include rhythm "kicks" and the more "catchy" introductions that are an essential part of the song. However, start simply, neatly, and accurately for easy readability. Your objective is for the lead sheet to be self-explanatory and capable of being read perfectly—on sight.

The Songbook

Your collection of lead sheets should be placed in a binder to create your songbook, which should include:

1. a tune list, with keys and broken down by style
2. charts or lead sheets in alphabetical order, with alphabetical tabs

It's a good idea to have a separate lyric book from which you can subtly glance at lyrics from a distance. You might also include the composer and lyricist as well as the original recording artist and/or musical from which the song is taken. This information serves as a valuable resource when preparing medleys or verbal introductions.

Lead Sheet Checklist

1. *Paper*	Heavy enough not to fall off piano!
2. *Song Title*	Centered, bold, and underlined
3. *Composer & Lyricist*	In that order. Listing information such as the musical from which the song originates helps in forming and introducing song medleys
4. *Instrument*	Upper right-hand corner.
5. *Introduction*	Vamp or specific melody line with chords. Remember! Think in phrases of 4-8-12-16
6. *Rehearsal Letters*	Capital A-B-C, etc., within a square bold enough to stand out. Denotes a section (verse, bridge) of the song and is a logical restarting point during rehearsals

FIGURE 2.1 Legend for numbers in figure: 1. *Title* is bold and centered; 2. *Composer and lyricist*; 3. Note *Style* (Swing) above first staff. Instrument is used in upper right-hand corner when there are arrangements for individual instruments; 4. Note *Rehearsal Letter*, bold and within the square. A third rehearsal letter (letter C) could have been used in measure 18. Rehearsal letters are very important in

7. *Chord Slashes*	Slanted, between 2nd and 4th line of staff. Spaced according to beats per measure
8. *Neatness of*	*Melody:* Use ruler for beams
	Lyrics: Use ruler and align with notes
	Spacing: Generally 4 measures per staff
9. *Form Markings & Repeat Signs*	Emphasize repeat signs with brackets. Verify the number of measures
D.S. Al Coda	Verify number of measures. Use bold markings
10. *Endings*	Set-up endings: Possible approaches:
	1. last phrase repeated 3 times
	2. rubato ending (ballads) with many fermatas
	3. tag, using deceptive cadence (VI chord)

CRITICAL LISTENING

Critical listening and appreciation for vocalists *and* instrumentalists who represent a broad spectrum of musical styles are invaluable, if not essential to developing one's own individual style. They also provide a deeper understanding of the elements that constitute specific vocal and musical styles and idioms as well as their development over time.

In discussing their "axe," instrumentalists seem to be able to compare different musical renditions of a particular tune, citing specific recordings by various artists and identifying *all* the personnel on the recording.

---

extended arrangements; 5. *Vamp Intro* would probably include the first four chords, using one chord per measure; 6. Note neatness of chords. Be consistent with chord symbols (e.g., triangle for major 7 and horizontal line for minor 7 are used here). Note also that the *chord extensions* are smaller than the chord letter—no lower than the upper half; 7. *Chord slashes* are not necessary for split measures or single-chord measures, but are necessary for three-chord measures; 8. *Alignment of lyrics with melody* is important. When copied manually, use a guideline to keep lyrics straight and neat; 9. Note the *heavy repeat* signs (bracket them if copying manually). If copying manually, it is neater to connect both staves rather than merely bracketing them. *Repeat signs* at the top of the tune are not necessary if there is no written introduction; 10. Note the alternate chord changes at the *2nd ending*; 11. Note the augmentation of the melody (half-time) with alternate changes and a *fermata* at the end. If you choose *rubato* or to *ritard the ending,* this should be notated on the lead sheet; and 12. Note the "rhythm kick" written in measure 21.

Instrumental musicians also like to compare (sometimes at length!) renditions of a specific song by different artists or discuss the performances of a composition by the same artist at different stages in his/her career. Such incisive analysis keeps them aware of subtle musical distinctions and the evolution of musical style or idiom.

Vocalists need be no different. Prominent vocalists who have "stood the test of time" have gained that longevity because they demonstrate some quality or characteristic that is unique or special or that embodies a specific musical style.

In developing the faculty for critical analysis:

1. Listen to male and female vocalists as well as instrumentalists. Some singers confine their listening to fellow vocalists only.

2. Listen "in context"—that is, keep in mind the timeframe in which the vocalist is performing. The time period of a recording will greatly influence certain vocal and performing characteristics, such as

    • vibrato, embellishments, and the vocal qualities demonstrated

    • the type of instrumental accompaniment, which can range from full string orchestra to big band to electronic drum machines and sequencers

    • the level of recording technology, which can influence overall clarity and presence, whether the vocals were "live" or overdubbed, and the existence of electronic enhancement of the vocal sound

3. Listen to vocalists at various stages in their performing careers. For example, the vocal renditions of a young Billie Holliday in the earliest stages of her career contrast sharply with the recordings of her final years.

Vocal Analysis Form

The following is a format that can assist in exploring and noting specific elements of a performance. Be detailed and descriptive. To say that a vocalist "feels the music" is not sufficient in describing how a vocalist communicates effectively. A singer should be able to articulate cogently what distinguishes one artist from another, describing the artist with such specificity, that someone would be able to identify the singer based on your observations. Try to remain objective. Even though you may not like particular artists, you should nonetheless be able to critically analyze their strong as well as weak points.

Artist:

Song Titles: Composers/lyricists; review wide sample of artists work, from debut to established career to mature stages of professional development.

Album Title: Note artistic choices; image; categorization.

Recording Company/Record Number: For future reference; look for reissue on CD. Note if switching recording companies affected career.

Recording Date: Important to note age and stage in career.

Personnel: Note individuals who may be on a number of artist's albums; specific players that contribute to specific sound or rhythmic feel.

Tune Type: Style and rhythmic feel; swing, traditional, or contemporary ballad, bossa, rock, funk, etc.; straight-8ths, 16ths, shuffle, etc.

Vocal Quality: Hard to define and standardize, even among professional speech scientists, because they tend to be subjective by nature. Possible descriptions: clear, breathy, husky, bright, dark, dull, round, hooty, edgy, smooth, rough, harsh, pushed, relaxed, swallowed, whiny, tight, deep, piercing, harsh, full.

Vibrato: Rate: slow; rapid; wobble; bleat. Frequency: narrow; wide. Does it affect intonation (sharp or flat)?; present throughout sustained tones?; only at ends of phrases?; straight-tone only?

Lyric Interpretation: How does the artist "buzz" or emphasize words? Special pronunciations?: detached?; intense?; passionate?; intimate?; subtext?; uses irony?; sense of humor?; playful?; sarcastic?

Phrasing and Rhythmic Treatment: Back-phrasing (behind the downbeat); jump-phrasing (ahead of downbeat); hesitation; anticipation; delay; straight.

Melodic Variation: Patterns in alterations; octave displacement; approaches to pick-up notes; approaches to cadences; lengthening melody; contracting melody; substitutions for low or high notes; literal or "straight" interpretation; heavily ornamented melody.

Vocal Embellishments: Falls; slurs; scoops; breath slurs; grace notes; yodels; cries; flips; turns; accents; apoggiaturas; doits; shakes; trills; growls; scrapes.

Time Feel: Behind the beat; ahead of beat; "laid-back"; frantic; "on top of the beat"; "in the pocket."

Interaction with Rhythm Section: Interplay; quotes; imitation; dialogue; changes in texture; individual instruments.

Intensity Devices: How does vocalist build? Timbre changes at high intensity; use of colors and textures; emphasis on certain consonants; long-sustained notes; inflections.

Unique Characteristics: What sets this vocalist apart from other distinguished vocalists? How would you describe this vocalist to make him/her immediately identifiable to a listener? Is this vocalist distinguished by: Vocal quality? Embellishments? Phrasing? Type of material? Identification with particular idiom? Time feel? Association with other musicians (part of a duo, trio, rhythm section)? Association with material of specific composer or lyricist? Association with emergence of a specific style or genre? Longevity?

What Do You Think Is Special about This Vocalist? Why you may feel this vocalist is prominent and presented as worthy of discussion and analysis? Why you may feel that artist is overrated or underrated? Why you like/dislike this vocalist? Why you respond strongly to this vocalist, whether negatively or positively? Entertainment value or artistic contribution?

Comments: General reactions and observations concerning vocalist and recording/performance career.

THREE

Performance "On the Gig"

THE "CLUB DATE"

Club Dates or Casuals

While you are waiting for the big break, an ideal way to gain practical experience in singing and performing is by doing "club dates," or "casuals." While some individuals wrinkle their noses at the thought of doing standard gigs, but performing at weddings, parties, charity balls, and society functions presents the ideal opportunity to try out new sounds, learn new styles, and to just simply sing in public while subsidizing your career. Earning money while doing what you love is far preferable to waiting tables while biding your time. Since you are being forced upon your audience to some degree (unlike concerts, where audience attend especially to see and hear you), your ability to win your listeners over would represent quite an accomplishment—a barometer of your talent.

There are basically three types of "gigs": the society gig, the ethnic gig, and the top-40 gig. Each type implies a particular set of repertoire. The society gig is generally a fundraiser or benefit that is attended by a sophisticated, monied crowd. Therefore the musical styles will range from standards from the 20s, 30s, and 40s, musical-theatre standards (Cole Porter, George Gershwin, etc.), and tunes from the big-band era, with some 50s, 60s, Motown, and 70s rock/disco tunes sprinkled in. Everything is presented at a tempo suitable for dancing and the music is continuous throughout the evening (no stoppages of music, with breaks staggered among the band members). Medleys comprised of songs taken from the same genre or era may be strung together (for example, songs from

Cabaret, Mame, Tomorrow, The Best of Times, and *Hello, Dolly!*). Consequently, the ability to know your keys, and the ability to react quickly, are indispensable skills. Dance movement can be kept to a minimum, since you serve as background or part of the ambiance for the function, rather than being the center of attention.

In the ethnic gig, which often is a wedding or bar mitzvah, knowledge of ethnic repertoire such as polkas, Irish jigs, Italian folk songs, and Greek and Jewish dances is very important. For the top-40 gig, remaining current with the newest, emerging artists and the songs topping the charts is the focus. While it keeps your repertoire fresh because you need to constantly keep it updated, it also requires considerable vocal strength, the ability to move well, and also endurance as you strive to accommodate a younger, high-energy, dancing crowd.

Repertoire

The best way to prepare yourself for consistent employment, anywhere from New York to Los Angeles, Chicago to Peoria, is to prepare and develop a broad repertoire that covers you for any situation—tunes that are popular wherever you are and whatever the crowd. For an average gig, you should also have the following:

1. Microphone cable, mike stand, and music stand
2. A book of song lyrics, with composer, lyricist, year published, and, if applicable, the name of the musical from which it is derived
3. A tune list with songs listed by category and with keys (although song keys should be memorized as much as possible)
4. Songbook containing charts or lead sheets, though in some gigs there may be no reading
5. "Hot spots" or monitors are optional, since they are sometimes part of the band's equipment, or a professional sound company is engaged. However, it is a good idea to own them in the event that you are doing a great deal of top-40 repertoire. As we discussed in the section Vocal Health, the ability to hear oneself over electronic instruments is critical to avoiding vocal strain

I encounter many singers who aspire to successful careers but, when asked to sing or present repertoire, they are prepared to perform only four or five songs at performance level. Others sing over the recorded tracks of some artists, *with* the artists and never by themselves, never realizing how dependent they are on the recorded accompaniment and the stylistic choices made by the original interpretation. Thus they are "leaning."

Every time you learn a song on your own, especially a song that is out of your usual repertoire and style, you are growing as a vocalist, since you are forced to take a deeper look at the melodic and lyric content of the song, rather than just imitating. "Standard tunes" are standards because they have endured over a long period of time and have melodic characteristics and lyrics that have touched, and continue to touch, generations of listeners. Singing standards is an education in itself, and as you broaden your repertoire, you will gradually be acquiring an individual style as well.

A good repertoire list should include a wide array of musical styles as well as representative artists by category. A tune list might look like this abridged version:

SOCIETY/KEY	STANDARD/KEY	BOSSA NOVA/KEY
On a Clear Day/E^b	Misty/C	Wave/D
Just in Time/B^b	What's New/G	Girl from Ipanema/F
Bill Bailey/C	As Time Goes By/B^b	Meditation/G
Night and Day/C	Nearness of You/C	Desafinado/G_m
Cabaret/C	It Had to be You/E^b	Triste/F

CONTEMPORARY/KEY	MUSICALS (UP-TEMPO)/KEY	MUSICALS (BALLAD)/KEY
Ice Castles/B^b	Tomorrow/E^b	Memory/A^b
The Way We Were/A	Hello Dolly/G	What I Did for Love/G
Through the Years/C	One/B^b	Think of Me/E^b
(Current love ballads)	New York, New York/C	Every Breath I Take/B^b

50s ROCK/KEY	50s BALLADS/KEY	DANCES/KEY
Rock Around Clock/C	Blue Moon/C	The Swim
Johnny Be Good/E*	Blueberry Hill/G	The Mashed Potato/F
Rockin' Robin/C	Earth Angel/D	The Hustle
Shout/E	Smoke Gets in Your Eyes/E^b	The Monkey
Shake, Rattle & Roll/F	Blueberry Hill/G	Shout

Note: Unlike vocal standards, that are preferably placed in flat keys, rock tunes can be be done in sharp keys, particularly E, since that is a comfortable key for the guitar.

CONTEMPORARY BALLADS/KEY	CONTEMPORARY ROCK/KEY
Relatively new hits being played on the radio, featuring the latest artists or movie soundtracks	The latest dance crazes and rock artists

For contemporary top-40 gigs, it is important that you have at least one song representing popular contemporary artists. If a song by a particular artist is requested, you can substitute another of his/her hits if you don't have the specific song requested in your repertoire.

Some sentimental love songs ("Feelings," "Wind Beneath my Wings," "You Light Up My Life") appear to be permanent fixtures in the club-date repertoire, since they are oft-requested songs for weddings, anniversaries, etc. (much to the consternation of working musicians). Supper club or cabaret gigs incorporate more musical-theatre standards, with songs by Cole Porter, George Gershwin, Jerry Herman, Michel LeGrand, and Marvin Hamlisch, among others. It is a rich repertoire that is a pleasure to maintain and expand.

It bears mentioning that, while repeated performances of a song can be rather trying to musicians, the special performer can nonetheless manage to infuse energy and render each song in a musical way. After all, listen to what Ella Fitzgerald could do with the play song, "A Tisket, A Tasket!" The last people to know you loath a particular song should be your listeners. Find something to like within each song you sing, and, regardless of your attitude towards it, always give it your best!

Song Form–Song Structure

Because it is so important to acquire the ability to think "on your feet" and maintain poise and presentation during performances, the vocalist must always know where he/she is with the tune—in short, be aware of song form. When something goes wrong when presenting a tune, instrumentalists can more easily hide behind their instruments and the difficulties are less obvious. However, a singer stumbling and stammering in front of the band is far more visible, even if the music behind is chaotic. Therefore, one learns how to extricate oneself gracefully from "crashes" by taking the lead and "meeting" at a central point in the tune, usually the "bridge."

As a general rule, song structure is broken down into units of 4-measure or 4-bar phrases. Just as dancers are beautifully attuned to this 4-measure unit and are choreographed accordingly, singers must develop the facility for feeling music in 4-bar phrases, particularly at introductions and in songs taken at a very fast tempo. Two 4-bar phrases (referred to as a *period* in classical theory) become an 8-bar statement or section. For example, you might hear a musical director say "4-bar intro, followed by section A, 8 bars." Apart from the introduction, which is generally four or eight measures, the body or "head" of the tune is usually comprised of a 32-bar or 64-bar A-A-B-A format as follows:

A 8 bars	A 16 bars	A 8 bars	A 8 bars
A 8 measures	A 16 bars	A 8 bars	A 8 bars
B 8 measures	B 16 bars	B 16 bars	B 16 bars
A 8 measures	A 16 bars	A 16 bars	A 8 bars
32 measures	64 bars	48 bars	40 bars

Most songs in popular music have a symmetrical structure, with the number of measures divisible by four (4). The B section is usually referred to as the "bridge" of the tune. It is readily identifiable, since the musical material forms a contrast to the A sections, and frequently, a return to the musical material in the A section brings the song to its conclusion. Some songs feature an extended ending, in which the original melody is repeated but extended or modified somewhat for the ending (example: "Cabaret").

In the majority of performance situations the vocalist will sing the song through, an instrumentalist will improvise over the first section of the song, and the vocalist will "come back in at the bridge to 'take it out'." This underscores the importance of knowing where you are in a tune at all times, since the singer must be aware of the entrance into the bridge to end the tune. If you "get lost," the band will *vamp*—that is, they will play a 4-bar sequence or repeat a chord-change over 4 measures so that you can make your entrance at the bridge. Once again, your ability to feel music in 4-bar phrases will condition you to intuitively interact with the rhythm section and always "come in at the bridge."

In listening to song selections, acquaint yourself with song structure and learn to think in terms of phrases. The text of songs also conforms to a symmetrical structure, and combining musical structure with the structure of language through phrasing is the trademark of the singer who truly communicates the meaning of a song.

Speaking of communication and lyrics, an often-overlooked section of standard ballads is the verse, which for many songs sets up the body of the song and lends meaning to the lyrics. Classic examples of verses that complement the body of the ballad are "My Funny Valentine" and "Bewitched," both typical of the many ballads that derive from the rich musical-theatre heritage of the 20s, 30s, and 40s. By becoming familiar with the classic ballads from this era you can enrich your repertoire, since a number of them ("Lady is a Tramp" and "On a Clear Day," for example) have developed into swing standards as well.

Learning Vocal Styles

Swing

Vocal Quality. Edgy, bright, focused, with articulated attacks (think of a trumpet).

Count-Offs. Snapped fingers on 2 and 4. Very definite and emphatic count-off: "ah-one, two, ah-one, two, three, four." Use a metronome to establish definite tempo sense. Take your time and say the lyrics mentally before counting off.

Time Feel. Quarter notes are bounced as if they are notated syncopations; in particular, anticipations promote a sense of energy and bounce without being rushed.

Rehearsal Techniques:

1. should be able to swing using only the melody on "ah," pulsing the attack into each note like a trumpet. "Bouncing the breath" provides the "oomph," punch, and sharpness without sounding frantic. Use a metronome

2. should be able to swing the text, saying the words in swing. Attacks that are punched with the consonants rather than coordinated with the breath will sound rushed

3. if you are truly swinging, you should be able to slow the tempo down. Sometimes, one has the impression that they are swinging at a brisk tempo, but the tempo serves as a camouflage. Begin with a conservative tempo, then pick it up as you get comfortable

4. keep the knees soft, not rolled back. It's hard to swing when your body is stiff. Snap your fingers and loosen your lower body, particularly the knees.

Attitude or "Vibe." Generally, the attitude is assertive, definite—not ambivalent or tentative. The term "sassy" is often used

Musical Accompaniment. Relate to the rhythm section in order to achieve an overall cohesive swing feel. Some vocalists relate to the drummer (particularly the high-hat); others relate to the bass. The singer must always be aware of the downbeat to each measure, particularly at brisk tempos, and acquire a keen sense of form (4-8-12-16 bars)

Artists. Ella Fitzgerald, Sarah Vaughan, Betty Carter, Frank Sinatra, Tony Bennett, to name but a few. Also listen to instrumentalists!

Bossa Nova

Vocal Quality. Diffuse, unforced vocal quality, as opposed to the edge of swing (notice the timbres use by the rhythm section)

Time Feel. 8th-note subdivision. Note the straight-eighths on the high-hat

Count-Off. Count-off straight, even 4 beats or subdivide "1 and 2 and 3 and 4 and . . ." to dictate subdivision

Rehearsal Techniques. While somewhat understated, bossas can be deceptively difficult and challenging. Often the melody notes are extensions (9th, 11th, 13th) with wide leaps or chromaticism. Should be able to perform melody on a vowel as well as rhythmically with the lyrics. Legato phrasing—a flowing quality even with the awareness of subdivision

Attitude. Sensual, understated, intimate. Clarity and presence are important in conveying text. There is less accentuation, and the overall effect is generally more mellow. Vibrato appears sparingly and usually only on sustained notes at the ends of phrases

Musical Accompaniment. Mellow, relaxed, which is why bossas are often used for background music. It's a good idea to have a solid list of Jobim bossa-nova standards, because they are standard repertoire everywhere

Artists. Astrid Gilberto with Stan Getz, Djavan, Antonio Carlos Jobim

Standard Ballad

Vocal Quality. Warm, diffuse, unforced quality. Conversational

Time Feel. 4/4, but implying 12/8

Count-Off. 1-2-3-4—snapping your fingers on each beat in a circular motion to imply the lilting 12/8 feel

Rehearsal Techniques:

1. in slow ballads, singers tend to be uncomfortable with silence and try to fill in the gaps with sustained phrasing. It's important to take your time. Become comfortable with pauses

2. recite the text aloud like a poem or as a soliloquy. Great ballads are not wordy, but tend to be noted for their economy of expression. Hence almost each word is "loaded" with meaning and implication, and single-word or 2-word phrases are not uncommon

3. note the ebb and flow, tension/relaxation of the melody and language

4. create a background of events for the song in your head and be aware of a specific atmosphere and mood you wish to convey. The effective presentation of a ballad involves aspects of acting as well as singing

5. if a particular ballad seems to run in your head constantly, there's a strong possibility that you have an affinity for it, because it conveys something special to you. Develop a personalized repertoire of ballads

6. don't rush the ending! Use fermatas and rubato endings in order to set-up the ending for the listeners. Rushing through the ending leaves the audience hanging and feeling vaguely dissatisfied and cheated

Attitude. Very personalized and intimate. Since everyone will relate to a specific lyric in a unique way, lyric-oriented phrasing and styling enables you to personalize your rendition. Make definite decisions on what the text is implying; if you are ambivalent, this indecision will manifest itself in your presentation

Musical Accompaniment. "Solo-centered," meaning that the vocalist should not feel constrained by the accompaniment, but should feel rhythmically free to phrase, with the rhythm section furnishing the steady rhythmic foundation. Rhythm-section members may play-off each other, without getting in the way. Be clear about dynamics (notate them in the arrangement) and about what you are setting out to do.

Listening. Nancy Wilson, Carmen McRae, Tony Bennett, to name but a few

Contemporary Ballad

Vocal Quality. Tends to be aggressive, assertive, intense. Vocal effects such as grunts, growls, rasp

Time Feel. 8th-note or 16th-note subdivision. Funk ballads characterized by dotted rather than straight-8ths, with strong backbeat (on beats 2 and 4). It is important to feel outer rhythm (quarter notes) as well as subdivision, otherwise time will feel rushed or frantic

Count-Off. For straight-8ths: "1 and 2 and 3 and 4 and . . ."; for funk: "1 and a 2 and a 3 and a 4" to define dotted feel, or use percussive sounds to emphasize subdivision, with strong downbeats

Rehearsal Techniques:

1. the majority of ballads are intimate and understated at the outset. In order to allow for more contrast, start conservatively in terms of dynamics and intensity so that the ballad can build up to the climax. Starting off too heavily weakens the impact
2. if the intensity level is consistent throughout the song, make use of changes in texture and density; for example, start with a single instrument, adding instruments as you build. To avoid monotony, change densities and use dynamics so that the song arrangement has form and direction
3. less opportunity for original phrasing, since one is somewhat constrained by the rhythmic pulse and juxtaposition of lyrics with melody to accommodate the rhythmic groove. Important words are highlighted through vocal inflections, ornamentation, or vocal effects

Attitude. Less understated, broader, and "bigger" than the understated cabaret or traditional ballad. Presentation overall must be more emphatic and aggressive at the outset

Musical Accompaniment. Electric guitars contribute to backup that is loud and aggressive. Competing with electronic technology (syths, drum machines, sequencers) necessitates increased projection throughout

Listening. Try to "track" one specific instrument throughout a recording, observing how it contributes to the groove, and also devices that build intensity and subtle variations within sections of the tune

Rock

Vocal Quality. Aggressive, edgy, vocal effects such as growls, rasp, yells, etc. Absence of vibrato. Must project over electronics

Time Feel. Straight quartet notes; frequently, ostinato bass-pattern, guitar riff, or keyboards establish a distinctive groove

Count-Offs. Count-offs and cut-offs are very large and part of the presentation

Rehearsal Techniques:

1. vocal technique is important when competing with loud backup. Initiation must be with a breath pulse, producing a sharp attack that helps cut through the wall of sound. Avoid hard glottal attacks on initial vowels, which cuts-off coordination with the breath. Avoid lifting or jutting the chin when using a stationary microphone. Avoid compressing of the neck muscles in "bringing the song to your audience"

2. directing the sound to the microphone through mouth-shaping (oral resonance) also enhances projection. Experiment "on mike" to observe how the microphone receives the sound

3. consonants can be exploded more vigorously (even exaggerated) to enhance clarity and definition

4. be sure that you have good monitors. You will automatically push reflexively if you cannot hear yourself clearly (the Lombard effect)

5. pace yourself during rehearsals. Don't waste your voice while instrumental passages are being worked-out repeatedly. Build endurance, but remember— the human voice cannot compete with electricity! Know when to "mark"

6. use melodic variation to build intensity. When repeating a chorus, bring intense passages up an octave or use octave substitutions

7. rock tunes keyed too low will sound muddy, while in tunes keyed too high the voice thins out in the climactic passages and the full, robust quality is lost. It is *not* necessary to sing a tune in the original key, but in a key that allows your unique instrument to assert itself at high intensity

Phrasing and Interpretation

> A well-sung (performed) song gives the illusion that it has never been sung before and beyond that, that its revelations are witnessed and heard by an audience at the very moment they are self-revealed to the singer.
>
> —David Craig, *On Singing on Stage*

Phrasing

While some coaches regard style as a matter of embellishments and stylistic elements, "attitude" as the motivating factor figures prominently. Otherwise, presentations can become mannered and seem contrived. The most authentic way to develop a personalized style and phrasing is through the *lyric content* and *attitude* or *sentiment* as it is perceived and further implied by the melody and rhythm.

Here are some phrasing devices that enable the singer to think more spontaneously and maintain focus:

Hesitation (back-phrasing): Waiting a couple of beats after the downbeat of a measure before initiating a phrase. This element makes the text sound more extemporaneous, rather than planned. It also augments tension as the listener awaits the next utterance.

Anticipation (jump-phrasing): Phrasing ahead of the downbeat, implying a rush of ideas and emotions.

Buzzing the Words: Emphasizing a word by

- the manner in which you pronounce it, such as lingering on the voiced consonant "l" in the word *love,* or being deliberate in the clicking of a final consonant
- ornamentation—using grace notes, appoggiaturas, falls, passing tones, or other devices to embellish a word
- melodic variation to bring the important word out of the melody
- lingering on an important word—calling attention to it

Pauses: Music is time and space, sound and silence. At a workshop for a Jazz Educators Convention (IAJE), the renown jazz vocalist Mark Murphy suggested to a singer that he/she "design me some silence." Taking time and allowing meaningful space between phrases and words contributes to a sense of spontaneity, resembling extemporaneous speech. Pauses are particularly important during the verse of a song, since the verse (like a classical recitative) is meant to be conversational, setting up the rest of the song. Hence, the delivery of the lyrics should conform to the prosody of the text.

The Cycle of Breath—Rhythmic Breathing

Within the context of a song, singers get in trouble as they sing long phrases without replenishing the breath supply. Having run out of breath support and feeling rushed, they feel constrained to take a catch-breath, which

1. tends to be shallow and audible, calling attention to itself;
2. tends to draw in cold, dehumidified air, affecting vocal quality and position of the larynx;
3. tends to present itself at the most inopportune times—for instance, in the middle of a word; and
4. tends to throw off coordination of the body with the music due to the abrupt nature of catch-breaths, making it difficult to recuperate.

There is never any reason for a singer to be out of breath, particularly a jazz/pop vocalist whose phrasing can be tailored around breath capacity. Just as the prosody of language has natural pauses built-in, letting those textual pauses coincide with inhalation puts your body in synchronization. It also serves to isolate and highlight musical and textual phrases much more effectively. In addition, speech therapists maintain that after around 7–9 seconds of continuous speech, the listener automatically tunes out. This probably holds true for nonstop vocalism as well.

In "scoping out" a tune, isolating the text and reciting it aloud as a poem facilitates the noting of natural pauses, buzz words, and meaningful hesitations. These natural pauses would suggest ideal opportunities to inhale! Also, ascribing rhythmic values to breaths (for example, taking a "quarter-note breath") makes the breath rhythmic and keeps the body "in sync" with itself.

Our temporal sense becomes skewed when we have to catch an ill-timed breath. In actuality, it takes just as much time to take a catch-breath as it does to take a poised quarter-note breath. The relaxed, poised inhalation does not call attention to itself and offers the added dividend of being more manageable. Just as one catch-breath begets another, causing a vicious cycle, maintaining a rhythmic cycle of low breathing promotes vocal control and effective communication of text.

Being Decisive: Making Choices

As a soloist, it is essential that the singer makes clear choices regarding the overall mood, tempo, rhythmic feel, and phrasing of a song. If the vocal soloist is ambivalent and displays a sense of uncertainty, this insecurity will manifest itself to the background musicians as well as the audience. In many cases, if a vocalist is tentative and does not assert herself/himself in terms of phrasing, rubato, tempo, and other facets of style and interpretation, an experienced pianist, who often also represents the conductor or leader of the rhythm section, might "take over." By being unclear and/or indecisive, the vocalist has in effect abdicated control and artistic decisions to the rhythm section. A singer, therefore, must never display ambivalence, but demonstrate conviction and hence clarity in terms of the musical experience he/she intends to convey. Otherwise, the impact of the overall performance is muted.

Camouflage

Every vocal or instrumental composition, regardless of musical style, has a difficult section that represents special challenges in terms of vocal and/or musical execution. This section (often at the climax of a tune) can cause a mishap that can result in a loss of vocal control and confidence. In more traditional or classical idioms, the vocalist is somewhat welded to the phrasing and music *as written* and strives to adhere strictly to the perceived intentions of the composer. However, in the more commercial idioms, the singer has more latitude to alter phrasing in order to accommodate breath support, control, and range. The vocalist can make substitutions for pick-up notes as well as alter melody notes in approaching the climactic points of a song. Nobody need know that these alterations, which become very personalized to accommodate each singer's particular strengths and weaknesses, were made to camouflage a difficult section. The result becomes a more individualized and personalized interpretation that is less predictable and hence distinct from other well-known renditions. Having every musical passage "scoped out" and using camouflage so that climactic passages of the song are under control frees the singer from anxiety and allows the focus of concentration to be on the communication of text and emotion.

Achieving a Personal Style

1. Don't overlook songs that were originally performed by a male (if you're a female) or vice versa.

2. Change the tempo rhythmic feel (e.g., swing to ballad). This can add a fresh perspective to a lyric.

3. In learning a song, reduce it to its basic elements (e.g., break it apart). Evaluate the lyrics for special nuances in interpretation; examine the *original* melody (as written) before listening to renditions by other artists. You will have less of a tendency to imitate.

4. Use a solo instrument as backup, or arrange imaginative musical accompaniment.

5. After performing a song repeatedly, think of ways in which you can incorporate some melodic variations that highlight certain words or phrases. Phrase differently to keep the lyrics fresh (just be sure that your phrasing is logical, like speech). Generally, ideas may start presenting themselves after you have performed a song numerous times.

6. Be aware of the positive feedback gained from friends and audiences in determining which songs and styles get the most positive reception and are associated with you as a vocalist. For example, if you really "wow them" with your scatting or with ballads that mean a lot to you personally, keep that in mind when auditioning or preparing for an important performance.

7. Be on the constant lookout for obscure tunes that can be brought back to life with a new interpretation. Become a collector of tunes.

8. Affiliate yourself with a songwriter as a source of original material that *you* bring to life with *your* interpretation. Both parties can benefit from such an exchange.

9. Listen to a variety of vocalists, and extract ideas into a style that is an amalgam of your favorites as a point of departure. If you are at a loss for ideas, ask yourself "how would I sing this phrase?" This approach can help activate a flow of ideas.

10. An artist will have difficulty communicating or getting in touch with creative ideas as long as he or she is intimidated by technical elements and as a conse-

quence becomes distracted by them. A vocalist must have control of his or her instrument to the extent that he or she will be free to convey a wide range of experience and emotion. Keep your voice in shape!

11. Know the distinctive sounds and quality of your voice and use it to your advantage. Also, use a variety or timbres and ranges to give you a wider range of expression.

12. Don't underestimate the importance of your appearance as you perform a song. The involvement you display in performing can add or detract immeasurably to a vocal rendition. Appearance is becoming increasingly important—indeed considered by many as equally essential to the successful performance of a song. Strive to communicate visually as well as aurally.

Common Oversights of Singers

1. Starting a song too heavily, allowing for little dynamic contrast and opportunities for building intensity.

2. Same dynamic levels throughout the song, with no releases of tension—"throwaways."

3. Subjugation of lyrics to the melody.

4. Subjugation of melody to lyrics (rarer).

5. Over-preoccupation with sounding pretty and showing off the voice.

6. Inappropriate key for tune.

7. Rushing—not taking one's time.

8. Overly constrained with melody as written. Failure to embellish the melody occasionally to accommodate voice or for variety.

9. Failure to make decisions concerning the mood or atmosphere the singer wishes to convey (thus negating or eliminating unity of structure and logical but personalized renditions). You must know these things before you can communicate it to your accompanist(s) and audience.

10. Being confined to a specific approach to a tune, whether personally developed or "borrowed" from an influential artist's version. *Remember:* one is always free to experiment and keep it fresh!

THE RECORDING SESSION

Studio Singing: The Recording Artist

As an active studio singer you may be required to sound like a 40s big-band singer in one session, become a hard rock & roller for another, and transform yourself into a smiling group singer for yet another. During the 80s and 90s era of retrospectives and specialization, a studio singer might be labeled as high-energy rock or become associated with the sweet, sensuous sound of some jingles. Whatever the specifications, studio singing requires a high degree of technical proficiency and vocal flexibility, keen awareness of style, and the integration of these elements at such a reflexive level that singing sounds totally natural, spontaneous, and uncontrived. In effect, recording technology places the voice and the singer under a microscope, magnifying blemishes. Any vocal insecurities may manifest themselves by a lack of energy or personality—both crucial elements on tape. Indeed, their presence is the trademark of any successful recording artist.

Steady advances in technology are emerging at an alarming pace and are transforming the world of recorded music. Yet, amid digital sampling, the vocoder, synclavier, and other electronic innovations, the human voice as a solo instrument still prevails, at least for now. Ultimately, the majority of professional singers, whether striving for careers as recording artists, back-up singers, or jingle singers will be required to perform in a recording studio. Many successful artists initiated their career as back-up singers or studio jingle singers. The list of such artists is quite impressive, including Patti Austin, Melissa Manchester, Valerie Simpson, and Whitney Houston. Being "audiogenic" becomes very important, because the tape doesn't lie.

Expectations

The expectations of jingle producers differ widely from those qualities sought after by record executives. With a jingle, the vocalist can have as little as 25 or 30 seconds in which to capture the undivided attention of the television viewer or radio listener while "pitching" a product. Thus the energy conveyed by the voice and the image associated with the singer's attitude and sound is what preoccupies ad-agency executives in selecting their identifying sound—their logo.

Studio singing tends to be cyclic. Formerly, in the 60s and 70s, versatility and adaptability were qualities much sought after, affording a vocalist access to a number of sessions in a variety of styles. In the 80s and 90s the tendency for specialization appears to have taken over, with singers "type-cast" as a gutsy soloist or a sensuous singer or a group singer. In smaller markets, versatility might still enable the novice to gain entry into an inherently tight and competitive field. In larger markets, that commanding and unique sound becomes important.

Record producers and executives, on the other hand, are focused on the vocalist's ability to captivate and maintain interest. This ability is foremost to the record producer, because an artist has two sides of an album with which to retain the listener's attention. Although the visual element through the music video and websites is becoming a focal point in artistic development, the average commuter with a sophisticated car radio/CD system nevertheless continues to demonstrate an appetite for the unique and interesting singer, independent of the visual effects.

Since jingle producers and ad agencies listen for different musical and vocal characteristics from those exacted by record companies, some producers suggest that the professional singer prepare two demo tapes: one tape as a jingle singer to be pitched to ad agencies, the other as an original recording artist and directed to record companies. This is particularly relevant to the singer who is promoting original material as well.

Preparing the Demo Tape

The Jingle Tape

In general, a jingle demo tape should be *no longer than* 3 minutes and should be comprised of excerpts of selections that display the vocalist's voice, personality, and individual style to best advantage. Place the strongest material at the beginning of the tape, since prominent jingle producers, inundated with hundreds of demo tapes, are quick to decide whether a tape is worth their time after the initial 60 seconds. Include only the material best representing your voice and talent. If artist imitations or specific styles such as country and western are included, they must sound authentic and proficient.

The individual selections should be very tightly edited so that there are no dead spots that result in a reduction of impact. It is a good idea to sequence selections imaginatively to create a strong impression. Many producers seem to prefer that vocal effects and doctoring of the tape be kept to a minimum so that they do not mask the inherent quality of the singer. Most producer's ears are so acute that they can detect any splicing, punching in, or doctoring of the tape. If tape alteration is used to disguise passages that are weak, tentative, or lacking in energy or attitude, the experienced producer will still quickly detect such deficiencies. Besides, producers are quite cognizant of the vocal "toys" and effects at their disposal within the recording setting, so that raw material—that is, vocal quality, phrasing, attitude, and energy—is what they are interested in.

Devote Enough Time to Mix and Edit the Demo!

The final mix is crucial, and it is at this step that some vocalists sabotage their efforts. The levels should be uniform, with a minimum of tape noise. Have a DAT tape as the master, if possible, since there is minimal tape noise when copying or transferring to another format. With ever-advancing technology, cassettes are giving way to DAT tapes and CDs, so you should have all formats available.

For a vocal demo tape, the voice should be forward in the mix so that it attracts full attention from the listener. A poor final mix can be aggravating and distracting to experienced ears, deflecting attention away from the vocalist. The vocal sound and performance should be the essential point.

Packaging the demo is also important, since bright colors and/or a striking logo can be an effective way of drawing attention to it while additionally projecting a certain level of imagination and creativity. It is essential that the cassette itself contain the name of the vocalist as well as a telephone number (with a message service or answering machine for your own protection) in the event that the cassette or disk becomes separated from its case. The table of contents within the case should be clear and copies should be done in "real time," since vocal quality tends to be compromised when copies are made at high speed. It is not necessary to label oneself as soprano, alto, tenor, or bass, since it limits performance opportunity and labels the vocalist. Besides, a vocalist should cultivate the ability to read and sing not only the melody, but harmony parts as well, and develop sufficient vocal range to defy categorization on the basis of range alone.

The Artist Tape

The demo tape for the aspiring recording artist and /or songwriter will have different content and a different format from jingle tapes. Remember that record producers and executives, who are inundated with demos, are listening for uniqueness, originality, and the ability to maintain interest. Does the vocalist offer something unique—a different perspective? Does a market exist for this vocalist's style or is it too similar to an already-established artist? If the singer is introducing original material, one could argue that a negative reaction towards the material could affect the response towards the vocals. Conversely, in promoting original material, the producer may react negatively to the material because the vocal rendition does not engage interest.

To obviate such a conflict, you might include one or two originals in combination with a previously recorded song by another recording artist in which you are able to imprint a personalized treatment. Some producers maintain that a tape should contain no more than three songs, even for a song demo. If they are interested in hearing more, they can then arrange for a personal interview and live performance. Record companies routinely employ individuals who have the responsibility of listening to the myriad of tapes that are submitted to record companies on a regular basis. The ability to bypass the first hurdle is crucial and underscores the importance of including only the very best material on the demo. Packaging the demo imaginatively, like a jingle demo, with the pertinent information is also essential for an artist demo. Therefore use bright colors; include your name and telephone number in bold print; and include a table of contents and counter. (The "counter" is the device on a machine that shows by number where selections are on the tape. DAT tapes and CDs are already supplanting demo cassettes.)

Studio Protocol

The procedures followed within the actual professional-studio setting can be duplicated within the academic setting. These procedures will acquaint the student with the working environment, time constraints, and necessary concentration of studio recording.

There are two basic levels or categories of recording sessions: the *demo session* and the *master session*. In the former, the producer is competing or bidding for the music associated with an advertising campaign. He/she must assemble a package, which includes the jingle and "logo" to present or "pitch" to the ad agency, which in turn presents it to the client. Occasionally, the jingle might be written by one agency, or "in-house" within the ad agency or company, and recorded by another. In any case, if the idea is bought and becomes final, the material is re-recorded in a professional studio, incorporating any changes suggested by the client. In the ever-evolving world of studio technology, many producers now own sophisticated home-recording studios, equipped with the latest technological advances. Much of the preliminary or demo work is accomplished in home studios. The time factor is therefore not quite as critical, but important nonetheless.

Within the vocal-group situation, some producers employ a vocal contractor who hires the vocalists, assembling the right combination of singers for the particular session. In solo work, the producer generally contacts the singer directly, since he/she may have been used to promote the jingle to the advertising agency at the outset. Within the group-contractor setting, the individual vocalist is responsible, first, to the vocal contractor, who acts as the intermediary to the producer. The producer, in turn, represents the interests of the ad agency executive and, ultimately, the client. In the case of the vocal soloists, the singer usually answers directly to the producer, who conveys the concepts and preferences to the client. Hence the hierarchical structure or "chain of command" would be as shown in figure 3.1.

Whether a group singer or soloist, the professional studio singer must arrive *on time,* preferably 10 to 15 minutes before the appointed time. This enables the singer to relax and get one's thoughts in order. Arriving early also alleviates anxiety on the part of the producer and client. Occasionally, there is a delay while rhythm tracks are "laid down"; nevertheless, *time is money,* and arriving late is unprofessional.

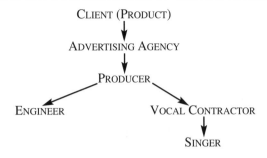

CLIENT (PRODUCT)

ADVERTISING AGENCY

PRODUCER

ENGINEER   VOCAL CONTRACTOR

SINGER

FIGURE 3.1 The hierarchical structure of the recording industry.

By the time the vocalists are called in, the rhythm tracks have usually been recorded. Sometimes "sweetening"—i.e., overdubbing horn tracks or strings—has also been completed. In certain instances the producer may request that the soloist record a quick "scratch" vocal track in order to give the client an idea of the overall sound. This also allows the singer to familiarize himself/herself with the style of the jingle.

Group Singer

In a vocal-group situation (assuming that the vocal sound has not been replaced by a synthesizer), the group then assembles in the recording studio. The singers position themselves according to voice-part or at the discretion of the vocal contractor or producer. The engineer also has critical input at this stage, since he/she is busy setting sound levels. This represents the ideal opportunity for singers to familiarize themselves with the music and assign parts, if necessary. The engineer will require feedback from the vocalists regarding the levels of equalization (also referred to as "live"), as well as overall levels of the rhythm track coming through the earphones. Each individual vocalist can also make adjustments on the individual headsets according to his/her own personal preferences, using the tiny boxes into which the headsets are plugged in. As the levels are being set, this is the ideal time to "clean-up" entrances, cut-offs, and resolve questions regarding the stylistic nuances, so that by the time the engineer is ready to record such mechanics have already been resolved. This is decidedly not the time for socializing—much valuable time and concentration could be wasted.

The engineer may also suggest positioning; for example, asking a singer to step forward or away from the mike in accordance with the blend heard in the control room. If any question arises regarding style, blend, levels, etc., it is the responsibility of the group leader (chosen by the producer or contractor) to arbitrate any changes or adjustments. This facilitates a more unified and consistent vocal-group sound and obviates time-consuming discussions.

Within vocal-group situations, it is of paramount importance that each singer maintain an upbeat, positive attitude, good energy concentration, and a "smiling sound." This is not always a simple task, after enduring repeated renditions of the same musical phrase. Some sessions can be especially high-pressure situations if the client, advertising agency representative, producer, and engineer are visibly conferring (at times heatedly) within the control room, while the singers can only look on helplessly and guess what is actually going on. Fortunately, with a strong, competent producer involved, most points of contention have been resolved before the master session and the producer is in full control of the situation.

The Head Session

In a *reading session,* which is becoming a rare phenomenon, the singer must internalize the elements very quickly and wean himself/herself away from the written music. Otherwise, the rendition is often "square"—i.e., lacking in energy and style. In a *head session,* in which most of the studio musicians may not read, the individual singers are assigned parts or sing unison lines that must be committed to memory for consistency and accuracy.

Enunciation, precision, energy, and style are the focal points of a strong vocal-group sound. The lead singer must be decisive and vocally strong, since the other vocalists will respond accordingly. In the head session, the music merely represents a point of departure for the ultimate product. The vocalist cannot be too literal at the expense of his/her "ear," since the result is generally a compromise in sound and energy. It is essential not to meld oneself too closely to the notes, since it is very likely that extensive rewrites will modify the original form and the vocalist must be alert to matters of intonation, blend, enunciation, and style, but remain flexible and professional enough to make modifications and take direction. For any session, the vocalist should always have a pencil handy in order to make notations on cut-offs, glottal attacks and other stylistic elements, and to make any needed alterations.

In the head session the vocalist must possess a superbly developed ear. He/she may be assigned a part, and developing a "personal shorthand" to transcribe that part can be very helpful. Many Nashville musicians have used this approach successfully.

Nashville Number System

Essentially, in the *Nashville number system* the scale is reduced to numbers corresponding to the major scale. For example, do-re-mi-fa-sol-la-ti-do becomes 1-2-3-4-5-6-7-8, with any accidentals being designated with a "#" or "b" (flat) before the note. The harmonic progression for a song, which has generally tended to be simple in Nashville, also adapts itself to a number system with the standard 1-vi-ii-V-1 chord progression notated as 1 6^{-7} 2^{-7} $2^{-7}/5$ 1. Slight variations are used, depending on the instrument and needs of the individual musician. However, such an outline serves as a valuable, time-saving device for the head session and also represents a good way to regard the major scale and melodies within the tonal functional system of Western music. The vocalist can accommodate it to his/her own needs without resorting to staff paper, or can place numbers representing the melody above the words on a lyric sheet. For example, notation can be reduced to:

7	7	7	8	7	5	3	1	2	1
You	can	make	a	diffe-	rence	in	a	child's	life

A harmony part might be notated:

7	5	5	6	5	3	1	5	7	3
You	can	make	a	diffe-	rence	in	a	child's	life

The advantages of such an approach are two-fold: It saves time, and it is flexible enough to allow for any alterations that need to be made quickly, without becoming bogged-down with musical notation. It nevertheless still furnishes a visible notation of the melody and harmony parts, so that singers do not "step on" each other by duplicating the same vocal line, which frequently happens when they are attempting spontaneous harmonies.

Reading

Strong reading skills are increasingly being subordinated to the ability of the singer to internalize a vocal attitude and sound quickly—the total picture. Some producers allow vocal soloists vast latitude in furnishing a stream of suggestions. This working approach largely depends on the familiarity and working relationship established between singer and producer. Regardless of working style, the ultimate decision of interpretation lies with the producer. It is the responsibility of the vocalist to follow suggestions and take direction, maintaining a positive attitude and high energy level throughout.

At all times, the professional group singer remains positive, upbeat, and responsive so that the performance level remains high. Many producers request a "smiling sound," which provides several positive attributes: First, the enunciation is enhanced because the tongue is automatically activated for pronunciation, and the brightness of the vocal quality is enhanced due to the taut lips and prominent teeth—hard surfaces that enhance high partial-energy. Enunciation becomes clear, the sound is bright, and in the words of Anita Kerr, "If you smile and think happy, you will sound that way when you sing."

In her book, *Choral Arranging,* Kerr, one of the pioneers of studio singing and arranging, succinctly describes the qualifications of a freelance, group studio singer (these qualifications apply to the solo singer as well): ". . . be ready to sing soft, loud, high, low, through your nose, with lots of vibrato, with no vibrato, edgy or mellow. Last but not least, read well, sing in tune, and follow directions."

Preparing for That First Big Session

Here are some specific steps in preparation for that big opportunity:

1. *Be available during the day when that all-important first call comes.* Have an answering machine or become a member of the Singer's Registry for easy contact. Although not having a day job can present a financial strain, being available when a session is offered is essential.

2. *Listen closely and critically to television and radio jingles and commercials,* remaining attuned to current trends in style and vocal qualities.

3. *Be knowledgeable about specific sounds and styles of the 40s, 50s,and 60s as well as prototypical artists.* Many producers and/or ad-agency clients use the names of representative artists to describe the sound they are seeking. This factor is particularly essential when "retros" or "remakes" are in vogue.

4. *Know contemporary recording artists and the state-of-the-art sounds and styles,* as well as representative artists and groups in *all* genres.

5. *Observe actual recording sessions* whenever possible to learn studio protocol and procedures as well as the working styles of various producers and ad agencies.

6. *Maintain contact at regular intervals with other vocalists and producers.* Participate in head sessions with established vocalists. In addition to being fun, they function as invaluable learning opportunities for fledgling studio singers.

7. *Practice and experiment constantly with the newest sounds.* Keep the voice flexible and responsive. This enables you to be comfortable and confident as you participate in actual recording.

8. *Maintain good personal hygiene and appearance.* Fresh breath is important when working in close proximity!

9. *Make yourself available for demo sessions or for recording original material by aspiring songwriters.* This provides invaluable hands-on experience.
10. *Maintain a poised, positive, and upbeat attitude* that makes you pleasant to work with and fun to be with.

AUDITIONS: MUSICAL THEATRE

Imagine for a minute that you have been given the responsibility of auditioning approximately 200 individuals for *one* singing job. Typically, you have been sitting in a room with few if any breaks for at least a full day (perhaps a day and a half), listening to a long line of eager performers as they give you their best. You try to accord them your fullest attention, but over a period of time, you begin to notice a pattern emerging on how you evaluate. You initially react to the individual's appearance: height, weight, proportion, coloring, age, and even "type." You form an impression about the auditioning individual's personality, professionalism, and attitude merely by the manner in which he/she carries himself or herself and how he/she speaks. How they relate to the accompanist, how thorough they are in the preparation of their musical accompaniment, and how courteous they are to the accompanist (is there a "Thank you"?) does not go unnoticed.

The first two phrases of the individual's musical selection will often enable you to categorize the voice, measure expression, preparation, communication abilities, individuality and thereby determine whether you need to hear any more. Finally, how the auditionee responds to your abrupt "Thank You" furnishes you with some idea about how he/she can handle direction and disappointment. All this within the timespan of 3 to 4 minutes!

What Are They Looking for?

When you audition for a position, whether it be a role in a musical summer stock, dinner theatre, cabaret, or supper club, the way you look will figure prominently in your chances of being hired—harsh as that reality may seem. We have virtually little or no control over our height, body-type, color of eyes, ethnic origin, and gender. We *do* exert some control over our hair color (?!!), proportion, and overall appearance. Since show business is just that—show—appearance becomes very important. In some instances auditioners are seeking specific types or are perhaps building a tall cast around their exceptionally tall leading man. Bear in mind, however, that even if you do not make the cut in a particular audition, having given a strong audition may impress someone enough to remember you for future projects. Thus every audition is an important one and there-fore always perform at your best. Also, it is important to keep in shape. Auditionees should be dressed neatly, with males in slacks and shirt, women in dress and heels.

Singer–Actor–Dancer

It is important for you to have identified your strengths and weaknesses in terms of the stage. Are you principally a singer who acts, or an actor who sings? Can you dance or do you merely move well, or is your leg/arm coordination a challenge? It is a good idea to acquire a realistic appraisal and *type* yourself as primarily a singer who dances, or a strong dancer who sings, just in case the auditions are broken down by emphasis. Be prepared in the event that the audition procedure requires all three—singing, danc-ing, acting. A performer should constantly be taking dancing, acting, and singing lessons in order to become a "triple threat," or at least to stay fresh and versatile.

What Are They Listening for?

If an auditioner is assembling a cast for summer stock, he/she needs a group representative of *all* voice parts for the chorus, with soloists capable of filling the major roles for that season. The season may include a tradi-tional Rodgers and Hammerstein musical, followed by a rock musical, a Sondheim show, and concluding with a little-known contemporary musi-cal. Therefore versatility on the part of the performers becomes essential.

In listening to a singer, the auditioner is listening for the inherent vocal quality, classification, projection, and range. Does the voice sound healthy so that it can withstand the rigors of rehearsals in the afternoon and per-formances at night? Can the singer convey the character and meaning of a song, or is he/she merely "throwing out the voice" or imitating? All these factors are being evaluated. Therefore the material you present should answer these questions while being packaged into a polished presentation.

Choosing Audition Material

A professional singer should always be audition-ready, that is, have audi-tion material prepared so that when an audition opportunity presents itself, you are mentally *and* musically prepared. Auditions sometimes come at the last minute, when you least expect them. One friend who appeared in a Tony award-winning Broadway show relates how one audition opportu-nity came on a holiday weekend, after she had just arrived from a month in Europe. She hadn't sung nor danced—indeed, had steadfastly avoided anything having to do with show business for a month, and here she was, being asked to do the audition of her life. Hence the importance of having at all times 16 bars, an up-tempo song, and a strong ballad *always* at performance level and with playable, readable musical accompaniment.

In selecting music for your audition, you should consider the following:

1. Does it show your vocal range as well as the "meat of your voice" to full advantage?
2. Can you relate strongly to the lyrics of the song and the character you are portraying? Could you conceivably be cast as this character? This is an important question. Some musical directors can take a song out of the context of the show from which it is taken, and are not bothered if a female sings what was originally a male character song. Others have less imagination, and performing a song out of context could work against you.
3. Are your selections in an ideal key so that the strengths of you voice are featured? If not, feel free to transpose them to a more comfortable key.
4. Can you do a very strong audition with these selections under any circumstance, even with a case of the flu or as you watch a celebrity walk in on your audition? Don't sabotage yourself by choosing songs that you can perform *only* when you are in perfect form. That climactic high note will seem much higher and keep you rattled throughout your audition.
5. Stay clear of frequently performed tunes. Some of them are ones that auditioners would really prefer never to hear again for the rest of their lives!

At some auditions you are requested to have no more than 16 bars of music prepared. The 16 bars you select should highlight the strongest part of your voice and be able to grab the listener's attention, with a strong ending. The piano introduction and ending should be minimal, because you want *all* the attention to be focused on you. Try to select 16 bars that are self-contained, that is, have a beginning, middle, and ending, with lyrics that communicate a complete idea. Examples of a strong 16-bar "c" can be found in songs such as "I Hear a Bell"or "All of my Laughter." You may also choose 16 bars out of a complete song that you use for auditions.

At most auditions you will be expected to have an up-tempo song and, for contrast, a ballad. An up-tempo song allows you to demonstrate projection, personality, energy, and aspects of vocal quality. The ballad presents you with an opportunity to demonstrate your ability to communicate the lyrics and nuances of emotion embodied within a song. It also displays your performance focus and ability to maintain interest. The ballad you choose should have a great deal of meaning to you, and you should thoroughly explore subtle shadings and subtext—treating it as a monologue with music. The voice in this instance is subordinate to the music, and your skill at bringing the listener *to* you and building up to a climax is paramount. Favorite ballads eventually become like old friends that you can turn to under pressure and that will pull you through because they evoke special meaning.

The female singer who belts but who also can flaunt a lyric soprano when called for should always have a selection taken from light opera, operetta, or soubrette musical theatre available in order to display your "legit voice." Also have an alternate selection that can be used to demonstrate the belt voice, if requested. It is difficult to display your vocal abilities with only one song or 16 bars if you are a belter but can sing "legit" as well. Under these circumstances, it is probably advisable to go with the sound that you identify with most strongly or that you feel fits the role they are looking for. You could also ask if the auditioning panel prefers hearing belt or legit, in which case the decision will be made for you; perhaps you will even be permitted to present both.

In addition to your 16 bars, up-tempo, and ballad (plus a "legit" standby prepared just in case), you might also wish to have a character song or "patter song" in your repertoire. After you've made the first cut, generally more time is allotted for auditioning, and you may be asked to display versatility and range. Having contrasting material available to present can help you demonstrate your variety. Nothing is more frustrating than being requested to sing something in a particular style, but not having all your musical repertoire with you. Bring more than you need—its better to have it and not need it than otherwise.

In another role-reversal exercise, imagine that you are the accompanist for the 200 auditionees for this specific job. You are relentlessly presented with a multitude of songs—some familiar, others not—that you are expected to play perfectly at first sight. Sometimes the copies of music are light and not clear; others are in large book collections that threaten to fall off the piano at any moment. Some pieces have instructions that are not well marked, yet the auditionee glares at you when you overlook one! On top of all, some auditionees walk off without so much as a word of thanks.

To get the accompanist on *your* side, present him/her with:

1. Music that is easy to read, clearly marked, and in the appropriate key (no transposition at sight).
2. Music that is straight forward, with no complicated introductions or interludes, no difficult page turns, and no built-in disaster areas such as unexpected modulations or confusing first and second endings to muddle through.
3. Neat copies of music in a spiral binder that will not fall off the piano, or copies affixed to cardboard backing so that they will stand upright. The pages are attached to each other accordion style, avoiding constant page turns.

Since you want attention riveted on you, avoid long introductions or endings that take precious minutes away from *your* audition. Simple accompaniments present less opportunity for distracting mistakes that blunt your impact—just the starting pitch will suffice in many cases. You also want to have the last say when you end your song, so just a "stinger" (a staccato chord at the end of your last note) or one measure by the accompanist is sufficient to punctuate the ending.

In the event that the piano accompaniment furnished at an audition is less than ideal, do not let it distract you. The musical directors that are auditioning you are just as interested in observing how you cope with the unexpected musical background and if you can perform with composure and confidence. If a performer is solid, with good concentration, problems with accompaniment will not affect a presentation. Do not give side-glances at the accompanist as if to alert the auditioners that a problem exists. It will not ingratiate you to the auditioning panel, besides being extremely unprofessional.

When you present your music to the accompanist, you should smile, introduce yourself, give any brief instructions for clarity, and nod when you are ready. Always thank the accompanist, regardless of the outcome. Accompanists are eager to help and render you the best accompaniment of which they are capable. The music that is well prepared will make the audition a much more enjoyable experience for everyone involved.

Performance Anxiety (Stage Fright)

Most performers have probably experienced some level of stage fright at some point in their careers—usually in the early stages. It is important to make a distinction between genuine fear of performing versus the excitement, anticipation, and sheer adrenaline flow that precedes that moment when you walk out on stage to greet your audience. The latter represent positive emotions that enable you to render an inspired and energized performance. The absence of these elements can even result in a flat or tight performance that is disappointing or boring to watch. Nevertheless, undue performance anxiety that consistently produces nervous symptoms such as sweating, trembling, over-salivating, sweaty palms, upset stomach, and uncontrolled gestures and movement needs to be addressed.

Extreme nervousness and performance anxiety will dissipate over a period of time as you perform more often and become more experienced on stage. You will learn that mistakes such as forgetting the lyrics of a tune are not unforgivable, and that the audience is far more generous toward such mishaps than you are. Every vocalist or actor has flubbed words—the key is not to get flustered or upset, but to be able to think on your feet. Very often your listeners may even be unaware that things did not proceed as smoothly as planned, and the energy generated by improvising or reacting extemporaneously can result in rather intense and entertaining presentations.

If performing on stage presents such a traumatic experience that it becomes debilitating and makes you physically ill, a reevaluation of you aspirations as a performer may be in order. After all, there is a limit as to how much one must "suffer for one's art." But if you experience moderate stage fright, the following steps offer some strategies to enable you to overcome it and establish physical and mental control during performances.

1. *Prepare and practice.* The best defense against stage fright is thorough preparation of material—practicing to an extent that your body as well as mind has internalized your material. This familiarity and "muscle memory" can only be achieved through constant repetition. As your body becomes increasingly familiarized with the sensations that you can expect to feel during performance, it becomes a much simpler task to maintain composure and poise during performance. Your body is not being assailed with a series of unfamiliar sensations, since you have acquired what is referred to as *proprioceptive* or *kinesthetic* memory, and it is much easier to maintain control. What many people believe to be stage fright is actually nervousness due to lack of preparation and practice. The inevitable result is a lack of confidence and security in performance.

2. *Use visualization and mental practice.* By visualizing your performance and going through it in its entirety several times, you are familiarizing yourself with the mental processes during performance. Don't succumb to the inclination to rush through the more difficult parts of your performance. This can be deceptive. Go through the entire performance step by step in "real time," so that when you are actually in performance you will feel as though you've been through it all before—which mentally you have!

3. *Use your adrenaline.* Don't mistake adrenaline and excitement for stage fright. The knowledge that some degree of nervousness and anticipation is natural is to be expected, and is in fact good for performance should prove reassuring.

4. *Stay positive and upbeat.* One misstep during a performance does not necessarily reduce its impact. Remember that you may have a clear idea of what you intend to do, but your audience will not feel cheated if you deviate and don't perform everything as planned. Some performers confine themselves into a performance that is so predictable that it lacks flexibility. They are also unable to think on their feet—a must in the world of the professional singer, who is often confronted with unforeseen circumstances.

5. *Avoid medication to combat stage fright.* The use of medications to combat stage fright is counterproductive for several reasons:

   • it never allows you the opportunity to overcome your performance anxiety naturally, through repeated successful performances (the best antidote), and

   • it engenders dependency by reinforcing the belief that you can only perform with drugs. You don't need them, particularly on a long-term basis.

Tips on Auditioning

What Are They Looking for? What Are They Listening for?

1. *Your voice:* range, vocal quality, projection, health
2. *Your physical appearance:* height, weight in proportion to height, age-range, "type"
3. *Your ability to sell a song:* How well you interpret and communicate the lyrics of a song, and how well you project a character. Would you be easy to work with, or do you have an "attitude"? How do you respond to your name being called?—first impressions are important!

Choosing the Best Auditioning Material

In selecting material with which to audition, consider the following:

1. Does it display your voice to full advantage—range, projection, style?
2. Can you relate strongly to the lyrics and character?
3. Is it in an ideal key so that the best part of your voice is featured? If not, feel free to transpose it into a comfortable key (unless you're auditioning for a specific show with that music).
4. Can you perform your selection under any circumstances (i.e., in spite of nerves; a touch of flu; while watching your favorite performer, someone whom you idolize, walking in on your audition; etc.)?
5. Is the piano accompaniment
   • playable at sight and clear, requiring minimum explanation, with no built-in disaster areas?
   • prepared so that it will not fall off the piano? (Use cardboard backing or a small loose-leaf binder.)
   • free of complicated and/or extended piano introductions or interludes?
6. Does your auditioning repertoire include:
   • 16 bars taken from a sing that displays you and your voice to best advantage? Sometimes you only have 1 minute—so flaunt it!
   • a ballad or slow song to demonstrate that you can maintain interest?
   • a belt tune or patter song or anything up-tempo?
7. For female vocalists, if you are a soprano, have something that displays your head voice, as well as something that shows your belt voice (if you have one and are comfortable with it).
8. Do not be afraid to use the same audition pieces for most of your auditions. Always bring at least three pieces, representative of contrasting styles.
9. Beware of the "special song syndrome" in which you feel a strong urge to substitute the "perfect," newly learned auditioning song at the last minute, only to sabotage yourself because you can't remember the words and don't feel totally comfortable with it. Stick with what you know and what works!

PART TWO

Teaching the
Commercial Singer

FOUR

$\mathcal{T}$eaching the $\mathcal{M}$icrophone Singer

The teaching of voice is a multifaceted endeavor, incorporating elements of acoustics, physiology, psychology, sociology, and aesthetics within the framework of exploring music as an art form. Vocal pedagogy is as rewarding as it is challenging, and much growth and knowledge can be derived from teaching others the art of singing. The purpose of this booklet is to provide you with the fundamental principles of vocal pedagogy that, combined with your individual background in vocal study as well as your professional experience as a vocalist, will better prepare you to teach beginning vocal students.

STUDENT-TEACHER INTERACTION

The Student

Each individual student who enters your studio is a unique composite of aptitudes, attitudes, and personal experiences—in short, a new psyche that responds to your instruction according to his/her individual learning style. Consequently, one of the challenges in training the human voice lies in the ability to remain flexible and accommodate to some degree each individual student's needs and manner of learning new concepts. For example, some students are very *proprioceptive*—that is, they are very aware of their body and the feedback of physical sensations as they sing. Other students may have difficulty in relating to this feedback, but possess the ear to imitate and quickly reproduce vocal qualities as demonstrated by the teacher. It is important therefore that the voice teacher remains cognizant of individual differences when imparting information to students.

There appear to be some popular misconceptions that students bring to their first voice lesson. A sample of these includes:

1. The perception that singing originates at the level of the larynx, since the vocal cords are in the voice box.
2. A preconceived notion about how they should sound. Usually, this idealized vocal quality is that of a favorite singer, who is imitated faithfully while singing along with the artist's recordings.
3. The perception that singing louder means pushing from the throat.
4. The perception that multiple tension sites (particularly, raised shoulders and chin and tight jaw) are necessary when "feeling" in singing. In actuality, such tension generally suggests ambivalence about opening up and outward in singing, and represent unconscious attempts to control and manipulate the sound as it proceeds out of the body.

The Vocal Instructor

The voice teacher inadvertently brings some preconceptions and weak practices to the voice studio as well, and these should be recognized in order to maintain objectivity. These may include:

1. The inability to acknowledge personal preferences and prejudices regarding different vocal qualities.
2. The inability to recognize differences in physical responses, while relating exclusively to one's own proprioceptive sensations. These may radically differ from those experienced by the student.
3. The tendency to pass along methods of one's own voice teachers exclusively, while ignoring alternative pedagogical approaches.
4. The avoidance of any vocal demonstration, or failure to use demonstration judiciously as a pedagogical tool.

THE FIRST LESSON

The following represents some suggestions regarding pertinent information that should be elicited from the initial interview, plus some steps in determining the performance level, attitudes, and ability of the student.

The following information should be collected:

1. Personal information: name, age, home?

2. Bilingual? Travel? These give the singer an opportunity to relax while allowing you to listen to how the individual uses his/her voice in everyday speech.

3. Number of years of study and nature of study (coaching, choral, classical, jazz, musical theatre).

4. Information regarding general health and physical conditioning, allergies, medications, major previous illnesses (if any), incidence of voice problems.

5. Note speech patterns and regional accents. Determine any previous speech therapy or training. If there are obvious speech problems, consider referral to a specialist. (Use a checklist. Refer the student to a licensed speech therapist if there appears to be long-standing voice and/or speech difficulties.)

6. Inquire as to what each student wishes to accomplish with vocal study. (What do they feel their problems and shortcomings are? What do they feel you need to work on?) Establish what their ultimate objectives are (performance, recording, media, etc.)?

7. Have the student sing, even though he/she may wish to vocalize. However, it is sometimes preferable to have them begin by singing a song with which they are comfortable for the following reasons:

   • it can provide you with insight on how the vocalist approaches singing as a whole

   • singing a comfortable song at the outset should enable the singer to deflect some nervousness and settle down into singing a tune. Beginning with vocal exercises may encourage the singer to get more "clinical and technical," particularly because it is natural to want to impress. One tends to place a burden on oneself in an effort to impress and perform perfectly when auditioning. Singing a prepared song not only demonstrates how the vocalist approaches the act of singing as a whole, but it also yields information regarding sense of style, musicality and sensitivity, and lyric-communication skills as well as technique, physical control, and overall body tension.

   • you may ask the student to sing a few songs in different styles (e.g., ballad and up-tempo), so that the singer avoids the feeling of being evaluated on just a short sampling.

8. If a student prefers to vocalize first, determine if he/she makes a habit of warming up before singing. If so, you may ask the student to demonstrate the warm-up regimen, which is informative and enables him/her to relax because of the familiarity of the exercises. Then have the student sing prepared material.

9. After asking any additional questions you might have regarding the singer's technical approach and style, it is helpful to both teacher and student to discuss:

   • what you as a teacher heard and observed as the vocalist performed. These elements should include positive aspects as well as negative ones and any potential problems that you feel might loom. It is a good idea to explain the reasons why

- steps that you would take to remedy identified vocal and/or physical problems and the teaching approach to accomplish these objectives, as well as your overall pedagogical philosophy (which need not be complicated!)

By gathering this information, both the teacher and potential student know "where they're coming from." This facilitates mutual understanding concerning the ultimate objectives of vocal study, thereby insuring that the student enjoys some sense of control and participation in developing technique and style. It also enhances communication and rapport.

LESSON FORMAT

Warm-Ups

The typical voice lesson should begin with a series of physical-relaxation and stress-release exercises, followed by vocal exercises and vocalizes designed to warm up the vocal mechanism. The length and extent of physical stretches and tension-release exercises depend on the student's activities immediately prior to the voice lesson and your perception of the student's state of mind. For example, driving furiously through rush-hour traffic while trying to avoid being late, combined with the daily stress of contemporary living, often results in a body that's wound up like a tightly coiled spring. It is well worth the extra 5-minute exercise regimen to release physical tension from the body, which will automatically manifest itself in the voice.

Vocal exercises and scales should build gradually from simple to complex, initially avoiding extremes in range and dynamics. There is actually heat generation associated with the friction of vibrating vocal folds within the larynx in the act of singing. Hence, the often-repeated admonition to avoid cold beverages during singing and immediately following rehearsals *do* have their basis in fact. Once the vocal mechanism is literally and figuratively warmed up by using tradition warm-up scales, a set of new exercises may be introduced to the student that addresses specific vocal problems or concepts.

The 20- to 25-minute exercise period might be followed by the performance of one or two familiar, fun songs for a period of 5 or 6 minutes. The rationale for opening up with comfortable repertoire (songs that are "old friends") is twofold: It keeps the student loose and coordinated while actually singing as opposed to vocalizing, and it allows for the application of technique within the context of presentation and performance. The student is then ready to explore less-familiar material and try out new concepts and technical principles.

Repertoire

A student's repertoire should include a number of selections that are the student's choice, combined with assigned tunes chosen by the teacher to address specific concepts and weaknesses. There exists a sufficient number of songs within each style to allow a student to build a repertoire from tunes that he/she has an affinity with. Simply stated, it is easier for a person to learn a song that he/she likes and sing it well. In addition, the teacher may also choose to assign specific tunes or styles of tunes designed to bring out or develop some technical element; for example, a rock tune to develop projection or a traditional ballad to work on phrasing concepts. A broad spectrum of vocal styles enhances versatility and allows for the application of different facets of vocal expression.

Record Keeping

It is important to keep a written record of each voice lesson, containing the following information:

1. Date and time of lesson.
2. Physical and vocal condition of student.
3. Warm-up and vocal exercises, including newly introduced vocalizes.
4. Major concepts discussed. These would include breakthrough ideas, new terminology, strong examples, and imagery that proved to be particularly effective. Extended discussion or topics of dialogue should also be noted.
5. Repertoire covered.
6. Assignments and deadlines for learning repertoire.
7. Level of preparation exhibited by the student.

To Tape or Not to Tape

As a rule, students who conscientiously record their voice lessons seem to demonstrate consistent and rapid vocal growth, in addition to improved insight into technical concepts. Recording the voice lesson enables the student to more-accurately recollect newly introduced exercises and vocalizes. Subtle changes in vocal quality are more distinguishable and monitored more objectively when recorded and subsequently analyzed. Audio tapes (and video tapes as well) can be reviewed periodically and repeatedly over an extended period of time, serving as a permanent record, thereby representing an invaluable pedagogical tool.

The Cool-Down

Following a session of vigorous singing or performing, it is wise to "cool-down" by doing some light humming or soft interval glides in order to relax the vocal folds. Just as dancers and athletes cool-down after rigorous exercise, singers should hum softly and perform yawn/sighs or very slow glissandos to relieve muscle tension.

CONTRAST IN STUDENTS' LEARNING STYLES

Dependent	Independent
Accepting; trusting	Skeptical; needs to test
"Just tell me what to do. I'll do it"	Needs to "try it on for size" before incorporating it
Teacher assigns repertoire	Prefers to choose own repertoire
Very literal; task-oriented	Needs to personalize as point of departure
Trusting; will follow directions without question	Needs to control and have some participation in establishing goals
Progress is slow but steady	Grows in spurts, with static levels
Responds to imagery; not interested in physiology	Kinesthetically aware; can tolerate mechanistic approach
Wants phrasing and interpretation to be dictated	Prefers to develop own phrasing and style
Typical Excuses:	Typical Excuses:
"I did what you told me"	*"This approach is not ideal for me"*
"Your directions weren't clear"	*"I don't do things by the book"*

The ability to identify facets of a student's learning style can facilitate the establishing of good rapport as well as enabling the vocalist to demonstrate good progress.

VOCAL EXERCISES

Stress-Release Exercises to Relocate Breath

We live in such a fast-paced society, it sometimes appears that we are all in a state of low-grade hysteria. Our body responds to the pressures and stresses of contemporary life by tightening up and closing-in on itself. The shoulders slump, the neck strains forward, the knees are locked, and our breathing becomes shallow.

The following is a brief regimen to relocate the breath to the lower part of the body and thereby enable us to become more centered. It can also be used when one is experiencing performance anxiety. Following this, the shoulders should feel comfortably lowered, the neck should feel free and "floating" (not compressed), the knees should be soft (not rolled back), and breathing should be low and unforced, with no shoulder elevation. If you have had neck or back problems, consult your doctor before implementing this regimen.

1. *The Roll-Up:* Bend over, knees soft, chin touching chest, and arms hanging heavily in front of you. Keeping the chin touching the chest, roll up slowly, vertebra by vertebra to the count of 25 or 30, *tucking in the buttocks* as you roll up. When you are finally standing erect, the *chin is the last part of the body* to be raised. Take a deep breath. Repeat. Remember to keep the knees soft (not rolled back), and *never* lift your head up suddenly from the rolled-over position.

2. *Head Rolls:* Look to your left, then roll the head *slowly* in a left to right motion, circling to the front of the body. Look to the right, followed by a circling motion to the left. Repeat three times.

3. *Neck Stretches:* Let chin fall downward, trying to stretch it to your chest without straining. Hold. Slowly let head fall backward as far as possible without straining. Hold. Repeat five times. Then tilt your head slowly to the right, bringing your right ear to your right shoulder. Pause, then bring left ear to left shoulder and hold. Repeat five times.

4. *Shoulder Rolls:* Roll your shoulders in a circular motion forward, then back. Repeat. Lift your shoulders to your ears (as if in a big shrug), then drop. Repeat.

5. *Arm Swings:* Swing your arms forward, then back, keeping your elbows soft. Swing your arms towards your body, "hugging yourself," then out again. Do arm circles in a forward motion, keeping your elbows soft, then reverse motion.

6. *Deep Breathing:* Inhale comfortably, but never to capacity or saturation:
   • inhale *slowly,* making a slurping sound through the mouth
   • inhale from the bottom up, feeling as though you are "inflating" from the lower part of the body first. Repeat
   • inhale *slowly* as if smelling a fragrant flower. Repeat
   • inhale *slowly,* feeling the air as it passes through the nostrils. Repeat

Car Calisthenics

We spend a lot of time in our cars, en route from one appointment to another in stressful traffic, most likely at certain hours to be bumper-to-bumper. Here are some simple warm-ups that you can do while driving (they may even help to settle your nerves!). Do not do these with background noise, such as a car radio, etc., because the tendency will be to push the voice.

1. *The Yawn-Sigh:* Sigh from the comfortable top of your range, downward in a slow, prolonged sigh. Repeat as needed.

2. *The Raspberry (lip flutter):* Allow the lips to vibrate, freeing the area around the mouth, and relaxing the lips.

3. *The Chewing Exercises:* Make chewing and smacking sounds as you pretend you are chewing a piece of toffee candy. Your mouth should move in an outward, wave-like motion, not just up and down. Do five "chews"; pause; repeat twice.

4. *Cleft Circles:* Place your finger on the cleft (hollow) of your chin and rotate in a circle. Do five rotations; pause; then repeat twice.

5. *The "Blow-Fish":* Fill cheeks with air, hold, then release. Repeat twice.

6. *Tongue Untied:* Move your tongue from side-to-side three times. Then move tongue up, behind top teeth, then down, behind bottom teeth three times. Then push the tongue behind the bottom teeth three times. Finally, move tongue in and out of the mouth, as with a bubbling sound.

7. *The Self-Centered Exercise:* Sing "ME-ME-ME-ME-ME" rapidly on a comfortable pitch, then on a five-note ascending and descending scale. Stay within a comfortable speaking range.

8. *The Cat Exercise:* Sing "MEOW-MEOW-MEOW-MEOW-MEOW" on a descending scale.

9. *Humming:* Do some light humming of a favorite song.

Attack in Phonation: Coordination with the Breath for the Initial Word of a Phrase

No matter how well the vocalist inhales prior to a phrase, if the first word originates at the throat with a hard glottal, it has in effect severed connection with the breathstream. Likewise, if the beginning of a phrase in a rock tune starts with a consonant that is pushed out rather than coordinated with the breath, the rest of the phrase will be localized in the throat. In addition, some styles, most notably gospel and country, have articulations into notes, the *breath slur* and *yodel attack,* that are synchronous with the onset of voice and are therefore categorized in this book as "attack in phonation."

If we continue with the paradigm of wind instruments, compare the trumpet attacks and phrases as they are generally used within the orchestral setting versus the jazz big-band setting. In the orchestra, the trumpet attacks are generally directly into the target note, with few slurs, flips, and

other indirect "articulatory" devices. The phrasing is smooth, with a continuous legato with straight tone or an even vibrato throughout. Within the
jazz big-band setting, the trumpets incorporate slurs, tenuto accents, and
other attacks into notes (called *articulations*), initially in imitation of
speech inflection and now part of singing in the commercial idioms as well.

The purpose of the following exercises is threefold: 1) To achieve
coordinated attack with the breath as almost reflexive, thereby avoiding
placement of the tone at the throat-level; 2) to coordinate enunciation of
consonants with the breath; and 3) to produce slurred and yodel attacks
into notes in conjunction with the breath.

Exercises for Coordinated Attack

1. Staccato with mouth closed (hum) on a pitch near the optimal speaking range
   - no air should escape from the nose
   - a natural vibrato should manifest itself on the half note if throat is open

2. Repeat exercise on [i] vowel

3. Do staccato exercise on [i] 1-2-3-2-1

4. Repeat exercise, altering rhythm to 6/8

5. Standard staccato exercises: 1-3-5-3-1; 1-5-8-5-1

5. Standard staccato exercises: 1-3-5-3-1; 1-5-8-5-1 (*continued*)

[a]

Exercises for Coordinated Attack with Consonants

1. Descending five-note scale, with notes detached

fa	fa	fa	fa	fa		va	va	va	va	va
pa	pa	pa	pa	pa		ba	ba	ba	ba	ba
ta	ta	ta	ta	ta		da	da	da	da	da
ka	ka	ka	ka	ka		ga	ga	ga	ga	ga
sa	sa	sa	sa	sa		za	za	za	za	za

		UNVOICED	VOICED
Fa	54321	fa fa fa fa fa	va va va va va
Pa	54321	pa pa pa pa pa	ba ba ba ba ba
Ta	54321	ta ta ta ta ta	da da da da da
Ka	54321	ka ka ka ka ka	ga ga ga ga ga
Sa	54321	sa sa sa sa sa	za za za za za

Note that: I. The articulators represent friction *against* the vowel and is attached to the vowel; 2. to reinforce this principle, precede consonant with vowel; and 3. be sure to isolate tongue from jaw so as not to overwork the jaw (use a mirror to monitor this).

2. Sustained [a] followed by the introduction of a consonant:

Ah		fa	fa	fa	fa	fa	Ah		va	va	va	va	va
Ah		ka	ka	ka	ka	ka	Ah		ga	ga	ga	ga	ga
Ah		ta	ta	ta	ta	ta	Ah		da	da	da	da	da
Ah		sa	sa	sa	sa	sa	Ah		za	za	za	za	za
Ah		pa	pa	pa	pa	pa	Ah		ba	ba	ba	ba	ba

3. Staccato consonants with [a] in a five-note descending scale:

fa	fa	fa	fa	fa

Exercises for the Breath Slur

The *breath slur,* derived from African-American gospel influences, is achieved through sudden flattening (contraction) of the diaphragm, resulting in a lowering of pitch and producing a *slur* or *scoop* into the note. This breath slur is differentiated from a regular scoop because it is aerodynamic in nature, initiated by the breathing muscles rather than in the throat. It is a distinctive slur or scoop into a note that is achieved through articulation of the breath in combination with the lateral expansion of the lower rib cage, particularly in the back. The upper body *must be* comfortably lifted and in extension, but isolated from the lower rib cage. There can be no upper-body tension or engagement in producing the tone.

1. To experience the sensation of the breath slur, pretend that something tastes delicious and you exclaim:

   "Mmmm Hmmm!"

   Notice the upward inflection and the corresponding down-and-out sensation and the lateral expansion of the rib cage, corresponding to the rise in inflection.

2. An alternative exercise to experience this sensation is to exclaim

   "Oh Yea!" or "Whoa!"

   as you observe something (or someone) that you especially approve of. Be sure not to rush or force the simple sentence. Once again, note how the lower rib cage expands down-and-out as the pitch rises.

3. *"Love" Exercise* (descending): Using the word "love" (you can substitute the expressions "Yea" or "Mmm" if these seem easier), descend the five-note scale slowly. Prepare the consonant [L] (tongue positioned behind the top front teeth), then let the vowel be sounded with the down-and-out expansion of the rib cage.

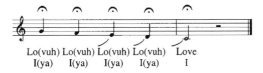

4. *"Love" Exercise* (ascending):

Exercises to Achieve the Yodel Attack

The *yodel attack,* sometimes referred to as a "vocal cry," "sob," or "flip," is heard within the country & western, folk, and rock idioms. It is achieved through yodeling into a note, in an "up and over" sensation. In the yodel, the note is approached from above with a yawning sensation, resulting in a voice break or yodeling quality as the voice flips-over at the initiation of a note. Viewed through videoendoscopy, the vocal folds close from the back, and the larynx immediately lowers for the sustained tone following the yodel. This "hooking in" is occasionally heard as used by tenors within the operatic world for the highest notes.

1. Sing the word "Hoo" or "Who," imitating an owl. The resultant tone should automatically be in falsetto or head.
2. Abruptly turn the word "Who" into the word "Wa." The shift from the closed [u] (which automatically places the voices in light register) to the open [a] vowel (which converts the sound to a full, open quality) results in a yodel or flipping sound. The result will be a vocal "cry" similar to that attack often heard in country & western-flavored idioms and some female rock singers.
3. The preparatory "Who" should be quick, breaking into the sustained open [a] vowel. Try these combinations: Who–Why; Who–When; Who–Where.
4. The shift from yodel into the target tone should be immediate and abrupt so that it is clearly an attack (or "articulation," as the term is used in jazz). The jazz-instrumental correlate is referred to as a *flip*. Physiological correlates:
   - the closed vowel [u] in combination with the explosion of air represented by the [h] ("Hoo" or "Who") results in a falsetto vocal quality (light registration)
   - abruptly adjusting to a bright, open vowel [a] or [e] shifts the voice to full voice (heavy registration)
   - for some individuals, using the [i] as the initial vowel and shifting to [a] abruptly will accomplish the same effect

Breath Management within the Speaking Voice

Just as the classical soprano will have notes in her range that are naturally more intense and project more easily in an acoustical setting, thereby identifying her repertoire and categorization (lyric, mezzo, spinto, etc.), the speaking range is also characterized by notes that are relaxed and full (with vocal folds flaccid), and notes that are naturally intense (with vocal folds that are stretched, with more tension). Knowing how to relax and allow the fullness of the low notes to assert themselves on the microphone, while maintaining strong support with an open throat for climactic, ascending passages in which the vocal folds assume more longitudinal tension, is an important function of breath management.

The objectives for the following exercises include: 1) achieving flexibility and agility ("bouncing the breath") through breath pulsing for shaping vocal lines as well as "runs" and other embellishments; 2) strengthening the lower back muscles in order to maintain low abdominal and back support; and 3) building intensity and support through resistance exercises while ascending the scale.

Exercise for Flexibility and Agility

1. "Follow the Yellow Brick Road": 1-2-3-4-3-2-1 on [i] vowel in 6/8 rhythm

2. Five-note scale on dotted rhythm: 1-2-3-4-5-4-3-2-1

3. Five-note scale on eighth-note followed by two 16ths: 1-123-345-543-321

4. Variation on five-note scale with same rhythmic figure: 1-132-243-354-321

5. Five-note scale, using triplet figure: 123-234-345-432-1

6. Staccato figure: 1-3-5-3-1 on [a] vowel

7. Staccato figure: 1-5-8-5-1 on [a] vowel

Exercises for Lower Back Muscles

Instruct the student to hum the exercises in a comfortable range to determine if the student is maintaining freedom at the level of the larynx. The student will more easily sense tension in the larynx when humming. Then proceed to vowels.

In the following exercises, the lower back is activated in a down-and-out motion, resulting in a raising of the pitch and dynamic level:

1. Interval exercise using lower back: 1-3-1-3-1-3-1-3-1

2. Interval exercise of a perfect 5th: 1-5-1-5-1-5-1-5- 1

3. Interval exercise of an octave: 1-8-1-8-1-8-1-8- 1

4. Repeat exercises 1 and 2 using dotted rhythms:

5. Ornamentation: Sing the following words rapidly—"Love," "Mine," "Me," "You," "Say"—using this figure:

Love

Resistance Exercises While Descending the Scale

Exercise for resistance in descending passages: 5-543-321 in a slow tempo, gradually increasing the tempo:

[a]

Registration: Singing Technique within the Speaking Range

Because much of commercial singing originates out of the speaking range, optimal voice placement becomes essential and underscores the relevance of optimal speech patterns, as discussed in chapter 1. In addition, key selection for song material becomes very important. Theoretically, the optimal pitch-range represents that range in which the vocal mechanism projects most naturally and freely. The section of the song that is most conversational and relaxed should lie within the voice range that is *naturally* relaxed. A natural fullness and richness of timbre will result because the folds are flaccid.

As the song builds in intensity, almost always with a concomitant rise in pitch-level, a natural intensity will result as the vocal folds assume longitudinal tension with rising pitch. Establishing countersupport with the lower back muscles, with a co-contracted diaphragm, keeps the larynx lowered and tension in the folds aerodynamically, without tension in the throat. It also produces depth or extensity of sound.

Exercises to Achieve Optimal Tone (Masque) Placement for the Speaking Range

1. Have student "meow" like a cat in order to feel the sensation of forward placement.
2. Around the passagio (lift), some singers find it useful to think of a "snarl balanced by a yawn" to prevent rigidity around the mouth.
3. Sing a five-note descending scale using "meow":

4. Using or [ŋj] before the [a] vowel can facilitate forward placement. Also, [m] and [n] have proven effective:

5. The [i] vowel enables the singer to achieve forward focus and placement and counteract throatiness.

Exercises for the Elevated Soft Palate

1. Initiate the beginning of a yawn with the mouth closed. Relax. Repeat three times. Remember that when we yawn, the back of the throat opens, *then* we drop the jaw. You may actually yawn while doing this exercise, which is good

as you open the throat. We also tend to inhale reflexively immediately prior to a yawn—so that is an additional benefit.

2. Sing an [a] on middle C (or another comfortable pitch) with a nasal quality, then gradually introduce a yawn to the tone. At some point you should sense the tone bouncing off the palate and projecting easily, with no sensation in the throat. Once the vowel is tuned, a natural brilliance and some vibrato will result.

Resonance: Vocal Tract Adjustment and Proprioception

We have already discussed aspects of *tone focus* and *palate positioning* as related to the speaking voice within the rubric of *registration*. Emphasizing optimally placed speech-range as opposed to the issue of chest or head register circumvents the necessity of dwelling on registration factors. The objective is to display singing out of the speaking voice that is robust, focused, open, and that projects effectively over the forceful instrumental accompaniment of aggressive styles.

On the microphone, the shape of the mouth and position of the tongue will balance the forward focus and give the illusion of chest voice and a deeper sound because of the fullness of the vocal quality. While in classical singing singers tap into the "singer's formant" and other acoustical elements to enhance projection, on the microphone the mouth becomes especially important as a resonator because of the mike's proximity effect and response to the sound source. (The exception is the head mike used in musical theatre, however, which does not transmute sound in the same way because the head of the mike is not directly near the mouth.)

This is why microphone singers should practice "on mike" as often as possible, because their instrument becomes the sound as it is transformed by sound reinforcement, and the effects of tone placement will be altered somewhat. However, microphone singing, like all healthy singing techniques, still entails placement that is away from the throat and coordinated with the breath-pulse.

Exercises for Tone Focus and Equalization of the Voice

1. Initial [ŋa] or [ŋja] to [a] on a four-note or five-note scale:

[ŋã]

2. Leap of a fifth or octave using initial [ŋa] or [ŋja]"

3. Chromatic scale on [a]. This has proven particularly effective in smoothing out the bridge in the voice:

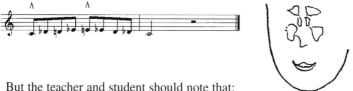

But the teacher and student should note that:

1. As the scale ascends, the lower and deeper the support.
2. Conversely, there is a sense of resistance and expansion as a musical figure descends, counteracting the tendency to collapse.
3. Be alert to the tendency to lift the chin with ascending pitch.
4. In the area of the "passagio" or bridge in the voice, the palate should be arched and jaw allowed to fall or drop, elongating the vocal tract and offsetting the tendency to lift the chin and compress the back of the neck.
5. Proprioceptively, there is an "up-and-over" sensation or that the tone "pops-over" suddenly.
6. Observations made by students experiencing this sensation as well as other examples of imagery that have proven effective include:
   • rolling up-and-over around the ears
   • reverse eyeglasses
   • directing the sound towards the roof of the mouth
7. Monitor with hands joined behind the neck or fingers on the nape of the neck to detect any neck tension or lifting of the head or chin. Note the following:
   • begin from an optimal pitch range at a medium dynamic level
   • as the scale ascends, use focus points to orient placement and resonance
   • imagery: Small elevator in the mask of the face that gradually ascends

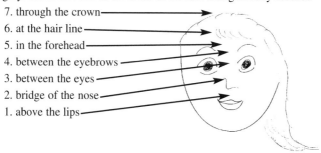

7. through the crown
6. at the hair line
5. in the forehead
4. between the eyebrows
3. between the eyes
2. bridge of the nose
1. above the lips

4. Avoid the inclination to use a uniformly loud dynamic level and pushing through the middle voice in an attempt to hear it as clearly as the other ranges. The softer dynamic level is an illusion.

5. Singers have sometimes tended to gravitate toward using extremes. Some employ an operatic head voice in which even vocalises begin in light registration, while others use a heavy chest voice exclusively, trying to belt or perform in the commercial idioms. The notion of a meeting ground that blends aspects of both extremes in the middle range is important so that the tone focus does not jump abruptly from the mouth and chest to around the forehead. If tone placement is too high for the middle range, the result is a sound that moves back and sounds muffled. Vibrato also tends to become obtrusive.

6. Suggesting that the middle-voice focus feels like a "snarl" sometimes will produce the forward placement required within the middle range for blend and balance.

7. Singers occasionally shy away from using forward tone focus in the mask of the face for fear of sounding nasal. Allowing them to hear themselves on tape can be reassuring in this regard.

Articulation: Enunciation That Maintains Coordination with the Breath

Tongue Exercises to Isolate Tongue Action and Increase Flexibility for Consonants

The tongue is extremely mobile and flexible, and its edges and body can move independently. The tongue does not contain many proprioceptors, so we tend not to have strong awareness or control of tongue action. The appendages and extremities of the body (the tip of the tongue qualifies as such) are the final sites over which humans gain conscious control, and the first to be surrendered as a result of certain forms of brain injury (stroke) or as a consequence of alcohol intake (witness the slurred speech of someone who is inebriated). When the tongue is lazy, the jaw tends to over-compensate in movement by flapping up and down. The purpose of these exercises is to become aware of different tongue regions as well as to isolate tongue action from the jaw, thereby increasing tongue flexibility and enhance clarity of enunciation.

1. Tongue flexibility for the tip of the tongue:
   - la la la la la   In doing the exercises, verify that the tongue is moving independently of the jaw
   - na na na na na   The jaw should not be flapping up and down
2. Tongue flexibility for the blade of the tongue. Verify that the contact between tongue and palate is not too far back, but that the stroke is in a forward direction:

- ka ka ka ka ka
- ga ga ga ga ga
- [ŋa] [ŋa] [ŋa] [ŋa] [ŋa]
3. Combination:
   - nunga nunga nunga nunga nung
   - dugga dugga dugga dugga dug
   - tocka tocka tocka tocka tock

Tongue Exercises with Vowels

The purpose of these exercises is to acquire proprioceptive awareness of the shape of the tongue.

Five-note descending scale:
[a] [i] [a] [i] [a]
[a] [e] [e] [e] [e]
[a] [ɛ] [a] [ɛ] [a]
[a] [æ] [a] [æ] [a]

The teacher and student should note the following:

- the shape of the tongue;
- if the tongue is comparatively wide or narrow;
- that if the tongue is wide and lateral, the tone quality can tend to be throaty; and
- that the tongue should move independently of the lips and jaw.

Vowel Exercises on the Microphone

Practice sustained vowel exercises on the microphone. Different tongue adjustments bring the sound forward, making it sound louder and more speech-like without lodging in the throat. Keep the tip of the tongue quite forward and firm as you pronounce the following words:

"SAY"   The tongue position is like that of the [ɛ] vowel and should be comparatively grooved and narrow.

"SO"   Adjust the [o] vowel so that the air moves forward into the head of the microphone. You will hear a crescendo when the vowel is tuned.

"SIGH"   Adjust the [i] vowel so that the tongue position is in the [a] vowel.

"SAD"   Again, the tongue is grooved and in the position of the [ɛ] vowel

It is a good idea to experiment with vowels and consonants on the microphone, because the mike "hears" sounds differently and certain adjustments produce distortion.

Coordination: Putting It All Together

Vibrato

The definition of *vibrato* presented by the distinguished acoustician and researcher Carl Seashore in the early 1930s continues to be cited to this day. He defined vibrato as "pulsations of pitch, usually accompanied with synchronous pulsations of loudness and timbre of such extent and rate as to give a pleasing flexibility, tenderness, and richness of tone" (Seashore, 1967).

Vibrato has been characterized as:

1. *Frequency vibrato,* which is oscillation in pitch
2. *Amplitude vibrato,* which is fluctuation in loudness
3. *Timbre vibrato,* which is periodic change in the strength of individual partials

Acoustical parameters of vibrato include:

1. *Rate:* the number of pulsations per second
2. *Extent:* the excursion of pitch modulation

Generally speaking, an acceptable vibrato rate lies between 6 and 7 cycles per second (cps), with 6.5 cps considered to be characteristic of the best singers (Large and Iwata 1971). As Sundberg (1987) suggests, 5.5 cps sounds unacceptably slow, while vibrato rates exceeding 7.5 cps tend to sound nervous. The vocal range of the sung tones influences rate, since warm passages that hover around the lower vocal range will manifest a slower vibrato, while energized passages in the higher ranges suggest a more rapid rate. (Notice the correlation between a trumpeter's or saxophone player's employment of a slow vibrato rate when playing a ballad, versus the vibrato rate used in dixieland, jazz, swing, or other highly energized tunes.)

Frequency excursion tends to be between a quarter-tone to a semitone, with the latter considered to be the most pleasing. Vibrato with a modulation of more than a whole step tends to be considered more like a jazz shake than vibrato. Vibrato should add vibrancy and richness to the tone quality, and vibrato that calls attention to itself or is obtrusive becomes a negative attribute. It also implies a problem in coordination of breath with resonance and placement.

Vibrato serves as a valuable aural cue of coordination. The following forms of vibrato represent problems in coordination:

1. *Lack of vibrato:* Suggests tension and stiffness, excessive glottal resistance, and lack of coordination with the breath source.
2. *Wobble (slow rate):* Suggests excessive body tension, particularly in the lower body, and excessive counterpressure, rather than allowing the air to be expired.
3. *Bleat (rapid rate):* Suggests "overblowing" (i.e., excessive airflow and insufficient glottal resistance).

Twist Vibrato. In swing and some Latin vocal styles (notably the bossa nova), the type of vibrato utilized is a subtle one that occurs at the very end of a phrase and consists of a very brief trill-like twist. It is produced by releasing the air and relaxing the musculature, resulting in a short trill at the release. It is found in music that is speech-like, with clipped phrases.

Wound-Up Vibrato. The "wound-up vibrato" is also heard only at the ends of a phrase, usually on a sustained note that begins as straight-tone and crescendos into vibrato for the second half of the note. Unlike traditional vocal styles in which vibrato is found in most of the sung tones within the phrase, as part of achieving a smooth legato, both twist and wound-up vibrato appear only at the ends of phrases within styles that are more "spoken" than sung.

Gospel Vibrato. The vibrato utilized within black gospel choirs is more of an *amplitude vibrato*—that is, an oscillation of breath pressure. It is characterized by a relatively slow rate and is frequently initiated with a breath slur. It appears not only at the ends of phrases, but also in pick-up notes.

Exercises to Acquire Vibrato

1. Staccato with mouth closed (hum) on a pitch near the optimal speaking range. Be sure to keep the throat open as the tone continues from the midsection and away from the throat.

2. Bouncing the interval of a major second: 1-2-1-2-1-2-1-2-1. The final note of the figure should have a natural vibrato:

3. Now dot the figure:

4. A 6/8 figure: 1-2-3-2-1

i

5. Sing this figure: 1-2-3-1-2-3-1

6. *"Twist" vibrato:* Ascend the five-note scale, using the following words— "Love," "Me," "You," "So," "Day," "Mine"—applying a tiny trill-like vibrato at the release:

Love   love   love   love   love

7. *"Wound-up" vibrato:* Sustain a note in your comfortable range and let it swell with the breath, applying a slight pulse to initiate the vibrato as the tone tapers off:

Love____

8. *Gospel vibrato:* Sing this musical figure, using the breath slur to initiate the tone:

L - [,]   [,] [,] [,]   [,] - ove

Straight-Tone Singing. There are some performance situations in which inhibiting vibrato is a desired effect; for example, in some Renaissance groups or some jazz styles. Straight-tone singing is usually associated with soft-to-moderate dynamic levels. In straight-tone singing, there is little glottal resistance to the airflow, resulting in a static, breathy quality. It is important to be aware of the distinction between allowing the airflow to pass through relaxed folds, versus pushing air through the cords, which is hard on the voice.

Some listeners perceive singing with diaphragmatic vibrato as sounding straight-tone because there is less frequency modulation. *Amplitude vibrato* (sometimes referred to as *diaphragmatic vibrato*) is used in group singing for the recording studio; it is easier to match the rate of vibrato and blend is easier to achieve because there exists less frequency excursion. The existence of amplitude vibrato results in a more vibrant, dynamic, energized sound while not compromising blend and unity of style.

Intensity Versus Extensity of Sound

Technically speaking, *intensity* is defined as "the objectively measured amount of power," whereas *loudness* refers to the subjective sensation of the magnitude of sound—how sound is perceived. (Radocy and Boyle 1979). In singing, however, the term *intensity* is often associated with a high level of feeling or emotion. A song passage can be intense without being loud; conversely, a passage can be loud while conveying little intensity. Intensity at a soft dynamic level can be very powerful and have considerable impact, as opposed to the predictable "blasting out" of a song. The ability to control dynamic levels contributes significantly to the impact of a song rendition.

There is also a distinction between *shallow singing,* in which there is no depth or support to the vocal tone, making the tone sound "anemic," as opposed to *soft singing,* which has depth and emotional intensity. *Extensity* of sound, which refers to the depth or fullness of sound, is dependent on maintaining the connection with the lower body, even at very soft dynamic levels. The singer must take care not to "let the bottom fall out" of the tone, even in the softest passages on microphone.

A vocalist not only should be able to project forcefully or sing very softly, but some styles (such as swing or pop tunes) require the ability to be able to sing at a medium dynamic, sounding casual at the outset before the song builds. The purpose of these exercises is to acquire dynamic control over a wide range with the breath, minus the harshness that comes with throat involvement.

Exercises for Control of Dynamics

1. Sing the following words over a four-measure chord sequence as if it was the final word in a song. Let the tone swell and taper so that it has shape and direction: "Love," "Me," "You," "Day," "So," "Mine"

2. Sustain a Bb or C freely and with vibrato in your comfortable speaking range, then abruptly open the lower rib cage. You should perceive a fuller, deeper sound, with extensity. Be sure to keep the upper body loose and isolated so that there is no tension.

3. Refer to the section on belting for additional exercises for projection.

Lyrical Exercises for Sustained Phrases

The following exercises are for achieving sustained, long lines (legato) while shaping the phrase. They are also designed to explore the upper register, using a more classical vocal quality.

1. Sing the following figure slowly and warmly over a four-measure chord sequence. Shape the phrases as if they were played by a cello, with broad strokes, maintaining engagement of the lower rib cage (side and back muscles):

   • 1-3-2-5-3

   • 1-3-5-1-3-5-1

   • 5-3-1-5-3

   • 1-2-1-3-1-4-1-5-1

Releases

Releases at the ends of phrases are a very important part of the rhythm of a piece. A good release will not only put a finishing touch on the previous phrase (think of it as punctuation), but also prepares you for the following phrase. Releases should assist your inhalation and articulation into the initial word of the next phrase.

Some singers and teachers advocate the *"puff-off"* or *breath release,* which can be effective since it tends to produce an automatic reflex to inhale following the puffed expiration of air. Within the vocal-group context, it can also help achieve coordinated cut-offs at the ends of phrases. They can be rather noisy, however, and if the song has a delicate, lyrical quality, the breath release can become a distraction.

In a quiet release, a slight breath-pulse coordinates with the release and should immediately result in an inhalation into the next work. It differs from the breath release in that there is no expired air. Releases should be rhythmic so that they do not call attention to themselves. It takes as much time to take a shallow snatch-breath, which can throw your rhythm off, as it does to take a quarter-note breath as part of the rhythm of the musical passage. (Refer to "The Cycle of Breath—Rhythmic Breathing" in chapter 3, p. 60.)

Developing coordination for releases:

1. 1-6-2-5-1

2. 11111-66666-22222-55555-11111

FIVE

Musical Theatre Pedagogy

In singing within the context of musical theatre, the ultimate objective is to express a character through song. Hence, the vocal quality employed, stage demeanor assumed, and attitude conveyed are all focused toward that end. Many songs within musical theatre settings are soliloquy or dialogue set to music. They serve the purpose of providing insight into a character's background and emotional makeup, thus establishing motivation for behavior. Clarity of enunciation, communication of text, and the illusion that thoughts and feelings are being expressed spontaneously without forethought are therefore of paramount importance. The beauty of the human voice is *not* the ideal nor emphasis, but rather the persuasive communication of mood, emotions, and personality through text.

This aspect of musical theatre performance has been an often-misunderstood or overlooked one by some traditional vocal pedagogues. Many an aspiring musical theatre performer has had limited auditioning success because he/she was too busy projecting the beautiful voice and displaying prodigious technique at the expense of lyric content and character. The voice should be at the service of the lyrics, each phrase uttered with clarity and credibility. Once the singer has internalized the musical and vocal mechanics of a song, he/she must go *one step further* to integrate the emotional content and characterization into the song as well.

OBJECTIVES

The objectives of musical theatre performance are as follows:

1. To be able to project the voice and demonstrate sufficient control and flexibility to accommodate the vocal needs of a broad range of songs and characters.

2. To be able to appear comfortable in his/her body (not stiff!) and to move comfortably enough while singing.
3. To be able to persuasively convey the emotions and motivations of a character through song (acting ability).
4. To be able to maintain vocal health and longevity within the contexts of strenuous rehearsal and performance schedules.

REPERTOIRE

There are divergent opinions regarding repertoire selection for musical theatre. These include:

1. *Emphasis on identifying "type"* that the singer falls into ("belter," "soubrette," "character") and preparing repertoire corresponding almost exclusively to that type. Some even suggest that in audition situations, singers should only use material that corresponds to their type and avoid roles that "go against type."
2. *Emphasis on versatility and developing a broad range of vocal styles and qualities.* Exploration of semiclassical, operetta, and any other style to which your voice is suited, including belting and character roles. The ability to be flexible and adaptable to a wide range of roles is particularly relevant when theaters are casting for summer stock or for the entire season using a small cast. A typical season, for example, might range from Gilbert and Sullivan to rock musical, followed by Sondheim or straight theatre and ending with a Rodgers and Hammerstein classic. Hence the ability to adopt varying styles and characterizations ultimately enhances employability. Additionally, broadening rather than limiting experimentation makes one that much the richer for the experiences.

Suitable repertoire might include:

"Legit" or "semi-legit": Selections taken from operetta or traditional musical theatre. This is the ideal vehicle to develop the entire range and cultivate the ability to project acoustically in large performance venues.

Ballad: A strong and expressive ballad provides the opportunity to communicate the text, mood, and characterization of a song as well as to display musicality. Ballads are an important and revealing element of the audition process.

Patter or up-tempo selections: These songs are ideal vehicles for developing clarity of enunciation. The "machine-gun" pace underscores the importance of understanding the prosody (rhythm, intonation, and stress) of the English language in order to facilitate communication of the text. Since patter tunes tend to be humorous and character-developers, poor intelligibility seriously undermines their impact.

Belter: A song that is forceful, proceeds out of speech, and gives the impression of popping right out of the mouth ("just belt it out!"). The definition and execution of tunes requiring belting is a controversial issue, but it really should be dealt with, since a number of roles require it.

Audition selection: Very short excerpts, usually 16 bars, which are always performance-ready in the event of unexpected auditions. This material should also be instantly available and playable by the accompanist at first sight (see chapter 3, "Auditions: Musical Theatre," p. 72). You would have one or two short excerpts available, as well as the other categories of tunes upon request.

COMMON WEAKNESSES OF ASPIRING SINGERS

These common weaknesses include:

1. *Sounding stiff.* Accommodating the lyrics to the melody rather than vice versa.
2. *Lack of clarity and intelligibility.*
3. *Sounding "trained."* This often-repeated criticism confounds some educators, but it refers to the tendency of some university-trained vocalists to defer exclusively to the voice and project beauty of tone as the only performance priority. While good technique and the ability to sing freely are essential, the pristine operatic vocal quality, vowel modification, and seamless legato characteristic of classical and operatic singing does not translate well to the clipped patter and belt tunes, nor to some conversational ballads.

American English has become increasingly halting and replete with inflection, as opposed to the legato line of European romance languages (and the English language spoken in Britain). Since we don't speak continuously "on the breath," but rather with many stops and starts (especially haltingly when we are conveying strong emotions), singing that is intended to convey extemporaneous speech should correspondingly be less legato, or the result sounds stilted and artificial. Hence the emphasis on attack and prosody within jazz and musical theatre styles, which are so closely aligned with the spontaneity and improvisation of speech.

BELTING

A Pedagogical Approach to Belting in Singing

While voice scientists and vocal pedagogues are still attempting to arrive at a common definition for the elusive term referred to as *belting,* students aspiring to professional careers as working singers within the musical theatre and recording industry continue to be asked to display a persuasive "belt" when they audition. Ultimately, it seems that it is the record producers and musical directors who determine whether the vocalist's belt sound and vocal productions satisfy *their* criteria. The formidable challenge for the voice teacher is to develop a pedagogy for belting that would enable vocalists to perform persuasively within a variety of contexts while enjoying vocal health and longevity.

How Belting Originated: Background

Belting in Musical Theatre

The confluence of evolving musical and theatrical elements resulted in a gradual introduction of new vocal sounds within the realm of musical theatre. These influences include:

1. *Demands of characterization* as sweet, lyrical soubrette roles, which implied pristine, virginal heroines and which were derivative of Western European opera and operetta traditions, gave way to more "gutsy" or earthy roles (Aldo Annie, Annie Oakley) in which characterization demanded spontaneous, unschooled-sounding monologues that were sung out of the speaking voice rather than being projected in head tones. One wonders whether Ethel Merman is cited as a belter because of the way she performed Mamma in *Gypsy* or whether it is cited as a belter role because Ethel Merman belted it.

2. *The interaction of African-American musical influences* as reflected in minstrel shows and vaudeville, in which the classic blues singers were required to project their voices outdoors without amplification, employing a shouted vocal production that emanated from the speaking range, reinforcing the change.

3. *The introduction of big-band instrumental accompaniments* as opposed to broad, legato string lines exclusively. The "popped" articulations by trumpets and saxes coincided with demands for more brassy vocal qualities and necessitated more-punctuated vocal attacks and just plain "oomph" for projection.

4. *Songs began to be keyed lower* (in flat keys) in order to accommodate brass and reeds as well as to permit the female character to project out of the speaking range, with no suggestion of technique and training.

Eventually, beauty and purity of tone became secondary to the communication of text within musical theatre, and vocal production became more representative of speech patterns. These conditions set the stage for belted vocal production.

Belting in Popular Music Styles (Microphone Belting)

The term *belting* is usually applied to singing within the musical theatre setting, but a second strain of vocalism was also evolving in the world of popular music. This stream was heavily influenced by electronic technology as well as the African-American musical idioms (blues and jazz). These styles, growing out of blues and the classic blues singers, were more rhythmically aggressive, with less legato, and proceeded out of vernacular speech with its strong articulation and inflection. At the outset, the invention of the microphone permitted more subtlety and crooning, but the gradual introduction of electronically amplified instruments (particularly electric bass and guitar) in rhythm & blues (and rock & roll, its Anglo counterpart) reintroduced the need to project over loud accompaniment to the extent that in the 1990s considerable projective power is exacted of the human voice if it is to assert itself as a distinguishable timbre (with text and clarity).

Yet another strain of popular-music styles, "hillbilly" and "western" or "cowboy" music (eventually consolidated under the term *country*), emerged as essentially folk music from the backhills of Southern states such as Tennessee, Georgia, and Texas. The vocal approaches were also derivative of speech, often flavored with gospel and blues influences. The vocal timbres included yodeling and voice "breaks" and "cries" and reflected the Southern drawls and twangs characteristic of the speech patterns of those regions. The accompaniments generally consisted of strumming guitars and/or banjo and performances were on microphone.

While the term *belting* is generally applied to singing within the musical theatre, it is also used within the world of popular music and recording as well. Just as classical vocalists developed vocal technique and pedagogy in order to adapt to performing acoustically over larger and larger orchestras and larger performance venues, singers in the musical theatre and popular-music idioms also developed strategies to cope with the changes in instrumental accompaniment, technology, and musical styles within the context of contemporary music. In popular music, the prevailing popular artists of the moment tend to influence the vocal sounds that are emulated, while within musical theatre, the specific roles *as written and performed* in the original production serve that function.

Arriving at a Workable Definition of Belting

The following definitions of belting have been proffered by voice scientists and researchers (and others):

> "The belt sound is a tense, tough, driving, bright, vibrato-less, assertive yell" (Boardman 1989).
>
> "In our judgment, belting can be described as a mode of singing that is typified by unusually loud, heavy phonation that exhibits little or no vibrato but a high level of nasality" (Miles and Hollien 1990).
>
> "Belting is a manner of loud singing that is characterized by consistent use of 'chest register' (less than 50% closed phase of glottis) in a range in which lar-

ynx elevation is necessary to match the first formant with the second harmonic on open (high F1) vowels, that is G4–D5 in female voices" (Schutte and Miller 1993).

"The loud, bright, yelled singing which Ethel Merman made famous" (Boardman 1992).

"Aggressive and extended lower register or chest dominant singing" (Edwin 1988).

"Inherent to many definitions of belting is the driving of the 'chest voice' almost exclusively beyond the passagio or break without lightening or shifting registers" (Rogers 1969).

Other words associated with belting include "blatant" (Osborne 1979); "nasal" (Estill 1980); "loud" (virtually everyone [this is a generalized statement]).

A workable definition of belting might be: vocal production that proceeds out of the speaking range, with the prosody of speech, and that promotes a sense of spontaneity and aggressiveness.

In the author's dissertation, published in 1986, the following female vocalists were cited by the subjects of my research (young female singers between the ages of 15 and 26) as being prototypical belters. It is worthwhile observing that the list might be quite different today and that new names would be added to the list as new artists emerge, and as new musicals become fixtures on Broadway:

Liza Minelli	Jane Olivor
Jennifer Holliday	Barbra Streisand
Chaka Khan	Reba McIntyre
Bette Midler	Olivia Newton-John
Patti LaBelle	Aretha Franklin
Ethel Merman	Madonna
Whitney Houston	Melissa Manchester

In a study related to the author's dissertation, the following are responses to the question: "What's the first thing that comes into your head when I say the term 'belting'?":

"A louder sound—a chestier sound."

"Strong and loud, but clear—not distorted."

"Chest voice—loud—not a classical sound."

"Singing hard—pushing in chest voice—*Annie*."

"Chest voice—loud singing—big voice—musical comedy."

"Broadway, but not legit—chest voice—more forward."

"Carrying the chest voice to the higher range—usually loud—not too much vibrato."

"Really giving it all you've got."

"I'm scared of the word—I really tense up. Whenever I try to belt or hear someone trying it, it sounds like they're yelling and pushing. I think of nodes."

"Pop style—Broadway."

"Loud projection—powerful."

"Loud, sometimes strident—a real musical comedy-type of sound."

"Musical theatre—very straight tone."

"Stretching chest voice up to where it should be head—screaming."

"Something negative—pushed—heavy sound."

The apparent disparity between concepts of belting can be partially attributed to the fact that:

1. Some definitions focus (delimit) belting to within the realm of *musical theatre exclusively,* while others broaden the scope to include recording artists and microphone singers.
2. Some definitions categorize belting as a very specific *quality,* as exemplified by prototypical belters and/or voices that are emulated.
3. Some definitions emphasize registration factors and *chest voice* versus *head voice,* underscoring the tendency to regard belting as antithetical to "legit" singing.
4. Some definitions refer to belting as *inherently abusive vocalism,* characterized by a very specialized and rigid laryngeal adjustment, along with the tensions that are generally associated with "pushing" and hyperfunction.

Is Belting a Vocal Quality?

Since belting was regarded as being diametrically opposed to "legit" vocal production in that it employed the lowest vocal range of the female voice rather than exploiting traditional *head voice,* there has been a tendency to dwell on *chest voice* (in contrast to pristine head voice), *shouting* (in contrast to legato), and *nasal and edgy* (in contrast to rounded and full) as defining the belted vocal quality.

A former student appearing in a leading role for a road production once sent me a newspaper review in which she was described as singing in a "folkish-belter's voice"! With all of the subcategorizations advanced to describe belted qualities ("belt-mix," "belt with some legit," etc.), there are some pitfalls associated with restricting the term *belting* to a specific vocal quality.

- *Not all musical theatre roles that entail some belted vocal production demand the same vocal quality,* since characterization dictates whether the vocal sound is brassy, low pitched, and mature (for example, Oolie/Donna in *City of Angels*) or comparatively bright, nasal, and edgy (Adelaide in *Guys and Dolls*). By preparing vocalists to produce an isolated, specified vocal quality (and one that, according to some pedagogical definitions, is inherently abusive as well), we ultimately may limit the type of roles for which a vocalist is suited (and hence limit performance opportunities). This is especially crucial when students are auditioning in theatre conferences of summer stock, where musical directors are preparing seasons that may encompass a wide spectrum of styles, ranging from a traditional Rodgers and Hammerstein show to a 60s rock musical, from Gilbert and Sullivan to Stephen Sondheim. The same holds true for aspiring artists who must display some range and variety if they can be expected to maintain interest over the length of a compact disk. Consequently, versatility and vocal longevity become important considerations, and in my experience, students who display such range in quality and style are cultivated quickly.

• *How does one describe "quality"?* The problem of developing specific descriptive terminology for vocal qualities is well documented, with standardization still far from being achieved. The term "vocal quality" and responses to vocal timbres is subjective by nature.

Another drawback to narrowly defining belting as a vocal quality is that vocal qualities that are demanded are constantly in flux, contingent upon new musicals that emerge (consider the scope of vocal qualities demanded for characters in *Miss Saigon* versus characters in *Les Misérables* or *Tommy,* not to mention the latest revivals. While, on one hand, there is something to be said for knowing and developing one's strengths or "type" for getting roles (e.g., typecast as "a belter"), it should not be necessary to altogether eliminate other possibilities in vocal expression.

Within the recording industry, the newest "hot" vocalist determines the vocal qualities that will be emulated for at least some time, and singers doing club dates are required to persuasively perform this vocalist's hits. Many young vocalists will come to the voice studio already mimicking their favorite artist. Popular artists also dictate the vocal styles and timbres of jingle singers as well. Therefore the vocal qualities exhibited by young singers tend to show trends (the deeper voices of Irene Cara, Donna Summer, and Melissa Manchester of the early 80s have given way to the higher, mellismatic vocalisms of Whitney Houston and Mariah Carey, as of this writing).

Finally, teaching to achieve a specific vocal quality can not only limit artistic choices in terms of expression (as well as employment), it may not permit for the retention of the singer's individually unique sound and vocal identity. Describing belting as a type of aggressive vocal *production* that proceeds out of *speech* (or the speaking range) may be a more workable and flexible definition.

Common Acoustical Descriptions of Belting

1. Formant tuning
2. High intensity (loudness)
3. High partial energy
4. Bright vowels

Common Qualitative Descriptions of Belting

1. Harsh
2. Edgy
3. Brassy
4. Loud
5. Nasal

Common Register Descriptions of Belting

1. Chest voice
2. Head mix
3. Pushed voice
4. Driving beyond the passagio
5. Shout, yell

Common Physiological Descriptions of Belting

PHYSIOLOGICAL ADJUSTMENT	CORRELATES WITH
Long closed phase	Intensity
High glottal resistance	Intensity
Low airflow	Intensity within the speech range
High larynx	"Edgy"
Tongue forward	"Edgy"
Chest voice	Speech
Vibrato-less	Speech

What Belting Is

Belting is aggressive, intense, loud, edgy, spontaneous-sounding, uncontrived sounding, speech-like (like controlled yelling or shouting), sung with "oomph."

Is Belting Necessarily "Chest Voice"?

The term *chest voice* is part of many descriptions of belting. However, when we talk of *chest voice* or *chest register* (a controversial term), are we referring to it in terms of:

1. *Acoustics*—as consisting of a complex waveform with a spectral envelope featuring high partial energy and high formant frequencies?
2. *Physiology*—as predominantly vocalis-muscle action, elevated larynx, long closed phase of the glottis and hence high glottal resistance and low airflow?

3. *Perception*—as being edgy, loud, brassy, tight, bright, harsh?
4. *Proprioception*—as feeling chest vibration; just "belting it out"; spontaneous, big, and full?

As Boardman (1992) states: "Although much remains to be learned about belting, the use of the term 'chest voice' to describe it only clouds and confuses the issue."

It is also doubtful that the original belters thought in such technical terms when they were cast in belting roles. Rather, left to their own resources to develop and project a character musically, they reverted to belting numbers *out of speaking voice and range,* as opposed to projecting *head voice and range.* It might be more accurate to regard belting as singing that proceeds out of the speaking range, rather than as representing chest voice exclusively.

Since traditional vocal pedagogy had tended to emphasize the development of female head voice almost exclusively, forceful singing that proceeded out of the speaking range represented a strong contrast. Comparatively little attention had been devoted to the speaking range or to the "middle" voice, especially as approached from ascending passages (the bottom-up). Some pedagogues avoided the range altogether, never venturing below the F above middle C. Presently, increased attention is being accorded to the middle voice as a transitional register that unites and blends aspects of both *chest* and *head* voice.

In Osborne's often-cited article (1979), he observes that prototypical belters who enjoyed extended careers appeared to display a significant degree of "belt-mix"—vocal production that enlists forward "mask" placement associated with the middle voice. One can hear this in such disparate artists as Linda Ronstadt, Whitney Houston, and Patti Lupone, as well as in Merman and Streisand. Such vocal focus, in combination with directing the sound out of the mouth, can furnish an illusion of chest voice, but nonetheless proceeds out of *speech*. If a singer's speech pattern was well placed, away from the throat, she would tend to transfer such placement in singing within the speech range. Conversely, a vocalist with a throaty speaking voice would probably bring that throat resonance into play in singing within the lower range, especially if belting.

Just as healthy speech patterns and stage speech incorporates forward placement in the *modal register* (the term employed by speech scientists to refer to "speech mode"), singing that originates out of speech must also incorporate correct tone focus away from the throat, even in the lowest frequencies of the speaking register. The close relationship between speech and belting and other forms of commercial singing underscores the importance of healthy speech patterns as a point of departure and consultation with a voice specialist or speech pathologist if fundamental problems exist.

Need Belting Be Abusive?

For a long time, the number of available teachers willing to deal with contemporary vocal sounds was limited. Lacking training and guidance, singers who were cast in belt roles or who were trying to imitate the hottest new pop vocalist resorted to techniques that were not necessarily the most efficient or healthy but that produced the intended effect. (In a published interview, Celeste Holm describes her audition for Aldo Annie where she is asked to sing "in a completely untrained voice, like a kid" (Osborne 1979). These inefficient strategies and the resultant harsh qualities are associated with belting, as if they are necessary to define the sound.

Prominent laryngologists have maintained that belters tend to have a higher incidence of nodules and other vocal pathologies, reinforcing the tendency to regard belting derisively. One possible explanation for this phenomenon might be that in the initial stages, vocal disorders resulting from misuse or abuse generally manifest themselves in the upper range, near the *passagio* (break or bridge in the voice) or in soft passages, dynamic subtleties and ranges of the voice that remain largely untapped when belting. While the classical-music world makes provisions for vocal rest between performances, eight shows a week or four half-hour-sets, six nights a week in smoky and loud environments are the norm for the more commercial idioms. Performers feel pressured and are loathe to admit they are experiencing any problem. Therefore gradually developing vocal difficulties may remain undetected until they have reached a relatively advanced and thus critical stage.

Some young singers with vocal problems have been heard to say that they thought the throat *should hurt after a good workout.* Evidently, an integral part of a pedagogy for belting must include explanations of vocal hygiene and vocal health in addition to convincing singers that they *can* incorporate nonabusive strategies and achieve the "oomph" and projection desired while not sacrificing or harming their instruments.

Belting must be regarded and presented as *high-efficiency phonation*—that is, it exacts tremendous energy, sustained projection and support, and thus optimal vocal technique, control, and efficiency. An integral part of belting pedagogy *must* therefore include explanations that foster knowledge of the vocal mechanism, awareness of what constitutes vocal abuse and misuse, and strategies to produce the vocal sounds that are demanded efficiently, with the objective of vocal endurance. Equipped with this factual information, the professional singer would be better able to deal with the pressures placed on vocalists, who are often made to feel that they are being "prima donnas" or are labeled as "difficult" when they are merely exercising good vocal maintenance.

Belting, whether within the context of musical theatre or rock, persists in contemporary vocalism and is demonstrated by vocalists who have enjoyed some measure of success and longevity. Singers who have been well prepared and carefully taught can also enjoy long and fruitful careers if they exercise care and understanding of their instrument.

Objectives of a Pedagogical Approach to Belting

Achieving a Natural and Speechlike Delivery

Speech is characterized by the elements of *rhythm* (rate), *intonation* (modulation), and *accentuation* (stress). The ebb and flow of language gravitates towards important "buzz" words and reposes (pauses) at the ends of utterances. *Inflections* (scoops, slurs, falls, ornamentation) are usually representative of style and individuality. Unlike classical singing, we do not tend to speak on a continuous stream of air, with natural vibrato (although we apparently do tend to speak to the end of our breath supply according to speech therapists). American speech has become increasingly choppy and halting, with a series of hesitations, stops, and starts, as opposed to the flowing legato. This is particularly evident in the declamatory and emphatic speech that belting implies. Hence the importance of deferring to prosody of text to achieve a natural, spontaneous, and speech-sounding delivery.

Achieving the Prosody of Speech

1. In order to introduce belting to a vocalist with no prior belting experience, select (or have the student choose) a short patter tune that the singer likes and that lies predominantly within comfortable speaking range. Transpose the song if necessary. At low intensity points, the song should lie near the relaxed spoken range and should contain only one or two climactic points that explore the upper range of the speaking voice.

2. Have the vocalist speak the text with conviction and projection as if it were a piece of dialogue. Many students shy away from this exercise as if they are reluctant to hear their own voices, but they must concentrate (recording these exercises is particularly effective), taking note of:

   • *natural pauses* that denote ideas and phrases
   • *important "buzz" words* that invite more duration and stress
   • *the prosody of the language*—rate, intonation, rhythm, and inflection

3. It is not a bad idea to require the student to transcribe the text on a separate

piece of paper and thereby learn it from memory. This step accomplishes three important functions:

- it forces the vocalist to examine the text independently of the melody, isolating the rhythm of the text and preventing subordination of text to music
- it uncovers some nuances of meaning, character, and "subtext" when visualized as text or poetry
- it facilitates the development of attitudes and motivation underlying the text

4. Have the vocalist increase the projection level, until sounding as though he/she can convincingly project in a very large performance venue. Verify that they are not:

  - *pushing from the throat,* with chin raised and muscles of the neck contracted as they try to bring the text to the listener. This is usually an indication that vocal onset does not proceed from the midsection, but at the level of the larynx
  - *using glottal attacks on words with an initial vowel.* Put an [h] in parentheses or have then slur into the word so that connection with the breath pulse is maintained
  - *fighting the prosody of the language.* If the vocalist is fighting the prosody of the language, the body is in opposition with itself and the sung text sounds stiff and unnatural. Therefore there is less sense of spontaneity and the singing does not communicate as directly

5. Have the vocalist sing the melody at a moderate dynamic level on a vowel, noting the following:

  - *contour of melody*—intervals; high points; low points
  - *gravitations*—important climactic notes and downbeats versus "throw away" pickup notes
  - *dynamics* as well as *agogic* (notes of duration) and *tonic* (peak high notes or sudden low notes) accents
  - *natural pauses* and *cadences* implicit within the melody
  - the melodic rendition should *convey sensitivity and meaning,* capable of standing on its own, *independent of the lyric*

6. Have the vocalist assemble the elements. More often than not, the contour of the melody corresponds to the prosody of the text, and both elements should fuse together naturally. A patter tune, which is really dialogue set to music, should defer to the prosody of the text and should be delivered as such. Singers sound stiff and have difficulty communicating meaning in the text if they defer to the melody or are especially literal with note values, applying uniform weight to every single note. Consequently, every single syllable is accorded equal weight (and thus importance) and sounds unnatural and stilted.

Exercise for Intonation and Inflection

In modulation of the voice (and in intervals within the melody), the higher pitch is achieved by the lower back muscles. To experience this sensation, say "Mmmm, Mmmm!" or exclaim "Oh Yeah!" The pitch rises, reinforcing to the singer the concept that it is unnecessary to raise the larynx to raise pitch or sing and speak with "oomph." Practice with these phrases:

"Good morning!"	"Forever and ever"
"Ladies and gentlemen"	"How are you today?"
"Good evening!"	"What a beautiful day!"
"Please sit down!"	"This feeling is indescribable!"
"Listen carefully!"	"Wasn't that something!"
"Surprise! Surprise!"	"Please listen carefully!"
"Finally, I'm finished!"	"Once and for all!"
"Once upon a time . . ."	"Anyone and everyone"

Achieving Intensity and Edge for Projection

In coordinated (staccato) attack the vocal folds are sucked together vigorously but do not touch (Bernoulli effect), providing the glottal resistance and reduced low airflow that corresponds to intensity. Hollien, Brown, and Hollien (1971, p. 74) suggest that "vocal intensity regulation within the modal (speech) register is related to aerodynamic forces rather than muscular changes." The more that technique relies on breath source to enact on the vocal folds rather than at the throat area, the more efficient and healthy the production. We must phonate before we vibrate. Only after the vocal folds have been energetically set into vibration (through pulsing) do vocal-tract adjustments filter the tone, influencing the depth or volume, roundness versus brightness, and other aspects of vocal timbre.

Breath pulsing and coordinated (staccato) attack furnishes the sharpness and edge sought by belters. The energy with which the breath sets the cords into vibration contributes to perceived loudness and sharpness, plus the high partial energy for projection. The coordinated attack eliminates the need for glottal onset (which most speech pathologists regard as vocal misuse) but establishes the "oomph" and depth as well as the sharpness that enables the singer to sound like she's "just belting out a tune."

The Word List Exercise. The singer is instructed to say the following words and phrases out loud, as if she were forced to project within an extremely large performance venue. Its purpose is to develop proprioceptive memory for *vocal initiation (attack),* which is generated from the midsection with the sense that one is "bouncing the breath." This diaphragmatic attack produces the sharpness and edge without benefit of throat involvement. Often, the speakers will rush and push the sound out in an attempt to produce the sharpness and edge. Eventually, as speakers experience the swell of the vowel aerodynamically and allow the articulation with the breath to furnish the desired sharpness and projection, they eventually trust that they do not need to "help it along," and disengage upper-body involvement. In this exercise: 1) say the single-word expression; 2) repeat sharply; and 3) repeat with modulation and inflection.

"Whoa!"	"Where are you?"	"Good morning!"
"Where?"	"Wait!"	"I love you"
"Why?"	"Whenever!"	"I need you"
"What?"	"Wherever!"	"Let's go!"
"When?"	"Whatever!"	"Don't go!"
"Who?"	"There!"	"Hey! "
"Hey!"	"What's wrong?"	"Jump!"

Avoiding Shifts of Intensity at Dramatically Climactic Points in a Song

When a tenor approaches the climactic high-note of his aria, the listener vicariously senses the precarious struggle against the fatal crack into falsetto that would destroy any semblance of intensity and suspense. The same is true for the belter, for whom high notes also symbolize peaks of anger, excitement, or other energetic emotional responses. Just as the tenor strives to achieve climactic high-notes with as much openness and freedom as possible, belters can "pop out" intense passages, provided that:

- *The tone is initiated and projected with the breath pulse.* The illusion of depth or volume of sound is provided by the expanded lower rib cage ("bracing") (Sundberg 1993). Estill (in her workshop) and Sullivan (1989) both use the term *bracing*—that is, the tremendous support in the lower rib-cage muscles and back—when they refer to the breath support used in belting.

- *The throat is open, with the palate arched and the jaw free.* While ultimately the larynx may be raised, it serves no purpose to instruct a singer to raise the larynx to sing. The high vertical placement of the larynx may be attributed as much to the tongue positioning in belting, which is generally more lateral and forward (with more firmness at the tip) than in classical singing.

- *Focus is in the mask of the face and not in the throat.* Many discussions of belting refer to a "whine" or "snarl" or "nasality" that contributes to the edge and in a bright vocal quality. Once proper focus is maintained, the singer can round the lips and/or elongate (yawn or arch the palate with dropped jaw) to produce a darker or more mature quality, if desired.

- *The proprioceptive sensation of peak notes is one of an "up and over" feeling versus a reaching up for or scooping to the high note.* While equalizing the voice at moderate intensity levels consists of regulating the airflow consistently and evenly in ascending passages, intensity in ascending belted passages is accomplished through inhibiting airflow while still maintaining the resonance vertical focus points in the facial mask. The higher the passage, the lower and deeper the breath support through lower rib and back expansion.

Achieving Communication and Clarity of Text

As was mentioned previously, speech text "travels" to the listener if the prosody of language is honored. The listener unconsciously filters out articles and prepositions and focuses on the important nouns, pronouns, and verbs. Therefore thinking in those terms when communicating the lyrics of a song projects the ideas, moods, and sentiments as natural and extemporaneous.

Since belted tunes (and pop tunes) are keyed (or should be transposed) to correspond to the speech range, this obviates the necessity for vowel modification except for words in the highest belt range, in which the tongue assumes an [ε] position (also cited by Estill [1980]). The tongue figures prominently in the timbres of commercial singing styles, because unlike the relatively narrow, grooved tongue of pure vowels, it tends to be more lateral and flatter for more commercial singing styles. This is consistent with the fact that these styles are derivative of speech patterns, particularly those out of the Southern regions. It is also strongly present in black gospel and other styles emerging out of the African-American tradition. (Listening to Aretha Franklin and Patti Labelle as well as country singers Loretta Lynn and Tammy Wynette reveals a "twang" largely caused by tongue position.

Careful articulation of consonants becomes very important for intelligibility and efficiency, particularly in terms of initial consonants. Misarticulated consonants, in which the vocalist engages the articulators to click the sounds rather than allowing them to become friction against the expired air, results in cutting off the breath supply and necessitates greater muscular exertion. Coordination of consonants with the breath, particularly at the beginning of words and phrases, is very important in allowing the consonants to explode forward rather than become imploded. A flexible tongue that operates independently of the jaw is a subtlety that is crucial in the effective but healthy articulation of consonants, particularly the plosives and fricatives.

In belting, *articulation* occurs twice: First, with the articulation or pulsing of the breath; and, second, with the friction of the articulators against the pulsed breath out of the mouth. (Coincidentally, within the idiom of instrumental jazz, the term *articulation* refers to the attack of an instrument into a note, whether indirectly through slurs or directly through staccato or tenuto accents, somewhat in imitation of the inflections of speech.)

Achieving and Maintaining Vocal Health and Endurance

In singing that proceeds out of the speaking range, selection of keys is important so that one can control the levels of intensity within that range. Transposition into more comfortable keys is now recognized as an important health issue on Broadway, since recent litigation was passed to control it. Microphone singers should also be aware of key choice as crucial to maintaining healthy voices.

Singers can be persuaded that they do not need to push and resort to heavy chest voice to elicit the sound their are striving for, and that there is also a more efficient way to achieve the same result.

Many professional singers within the musical theatre and pop-music idioms are loathe to study or have even been advised not to study with traditional voice teachers for fear of "losing their naturalness" and "developing a trained sound." However, if singers can feel reassured that the objective of the voice teacher is to assist in developing the technique and flexibility to perform in a variety of styles and contexts, while maintaining vocal health and longevity, perhaps fewer singers shall lose their instruments as they pursue their craft.

Danger Signals

The danger signals of belting are:

1. A pulling in the throat or cracking on high notes.
2. Chin lifted, head forward, and neck muscles bulging.
3. An abrupt break or shift in resonance and quality.
4. Throat resonance rather than mask resonance.
5. Straight tone only; no dynamic control.

Examples of inefficient and/or abusive belting and correctives are presented below:

1. Pushing from the throat
   - reestablishing initiation from the breath pulse
   - attack exercises and exercises for flexibility and pulsing
2. Glottal attack used for sharpness
   - substitute coordinated attack (staccato), which furnishes sharpness without the cords striking each other in approximation
3. Throat resonance in order to achieve a speechlike quality
   - establishing forward tone focus and placement
   - use exercises such as the siren exercise, "meow," "whining," [ŋ] or [ɛ̃]

4. Closed throat (chin raised, compressed neck muscles) as a result of trying to "bring the sound to the listener"
   - disengaging upper-body involvement (head, neck, upper arms, and shoulders) by relaxation exercises
   - encouraging gestures and walking while singing can also assist in eliminating rigidity and facilitate connection with breath source
5. Lack of intelligibility and clarity of text
   - tongue isolation and flexibility exercises to prevent overworking the jaw to compensate
   - coordinating of initial consonants with breath rather than pushing them out
   - deferring to the prosody of language rather than applying equal weight and emphasis on every note and thus every syllable of a word

Spot-Checking for Efficient Belting

Determine that the speech pattern is healthy, since it will be transferred to singing that emanates out of the speaking range. Consultation with a certified speech pathologist is recommended if there are any concerns. Verify the following items:

1. *Attack:* Diaphragmatic, articulated from the midsection, not initiated at the throat, or with a glottal attack.
2. *Posture:* Eliminate upper-body tension, especially in the back of the neck (raised chin), shoulders, and upper back.
3. *Intensity:* Not pushed, but having depth or extensity of sound.
4. *Resonance:* Tone focus is not in the throat (pharyngeal resonance) but in the mask of the face. Maintain open throat.
5. *Registration:* The quality need not be *chest voice,* but *speaking voice* that is energized with the breath and has proper forward placement.
6. *Articulation:* Consonants are coordinated with the breath, not pushed out by the articulators. Tongue flexibility and independence from the jaw should be established.

SIX

Coda: Preparing Yourself for Success

PREPARING YOURSELF FOR SUCCESS IN YOUR CHOSEN PROFESSION

1. Try to have substantial savings to tide you over when you move to a new city to pursue your career.

2. Have a few contacts or relatives to relieve the trauma of moving to a large, unfamiliar city. You might consider visiting the city for a week or so prior to your actual relocation in order to get a feel for it and its ambiance.

3. Have an answering machine, voice mail, or reputable answering service. This is absolutely essential! You must be available always and be easy to contact!

4. Acquaint yourself with names, agencies, publishers, studios, producers, etc., during your initial visit, so that you can refer to them later.

5. Obtain music-industry publications, visit union offices, local universities, etc. (even check the phone book!). The union offices of, for example, the National Association of Recording Arts and Sciences (NARAS), the American Federation of Television and Radio Artists (AFTRA), the American Federation of Musicians (AFM), and the Screen Actors Guild (SAG), to name just a few, as well as recording studios, are fertile places for announcements regarding auditions, available positions, planned group tours, etc. Local universities can also be helpful in this regard.

6. Make several copies of your demo (cassette, DAT, or CD for clearer transfer). Make certain that it is well packaged and labeled and has your telephone number on it.

7. Have your book and repertoire of songs and keys. Always have one or two songs ready that show you off and that can be performed *on demand,* probably without microphone. It needs to look and sound easy for you to do this.

8. Keep yourself in shape, healthy, and maintain a positive attitude.

9. Consider taking dance classes, acting classes, and university courses where you might meet other aspiring and working singers, actors, etc.

10. Check out clubs and night spots for working musicians and offer to sit in.

11. Call and make an appointment (if possible) to bring your tape to a producer, engineer, or publisher *in person.* Be persistent—that way, you are more likely to be remembered!

12. Audition personally for talent agencies that book gigs and club dates. Check with the local union if you are not sure of the reputability of an agency.

WHEN YOU'VE DECIDED TO "GO FOR IT"

Some Things to Consider

Demo	Make it a good one—one that is truly representative of your talents and versatility. Package and label it in a colorful way. Be sure that your name and telephone number are on the tape itself. Deliver it personally and try to get an interview if you can manage it Make two separate demos: one for jingles and one that displays your artistry.
Appearance	Shed excess pounds, particularly in these days of video. It is also important to look good as a backup singer. Remember, the camera adds 10 pounds to the way your frame appears.
Uniqueness	Both as a singer and in appearance. This means you have to have a good knowledge of yourself as an individual.
Acting Classes	These can help you understand yourself and help you "become" or "experience" what you are singing about.
Dance Classes	These can help you to move well on stage, which can be beneficial when you are auditioning.
Be Well Rounded	Learn another instrument. Become a "triple threat"!
Pictures/Resume	These can't hurt. Get them to a talent agency. Acting and singing are so interrelated that you might make contacts.
Demo Sessions	While gathering experience that is invaluable, your voice may also catch the ear of someone influential.
Songwriters	Get to know these people! They are an invaluable source of original material and demo work.
Names and Faces	Remember them! They may become important later on.
Industry Jobs	Get one of these to make contacts and learn about the business. They'll also understand if you have to go for an audition or session.

Open Sessions	Go to these to learn how some producers work and observe how it's done. You can also meet some interesting people.
Be Alert	Each city has its own particular way of doing things. Be employable in many markets by learning the operations of each.
Confidence	Develop it in yourself. You deserve the best and have worked hard for it!!

Above all, *Sing! Sing! Sing!*

APPENDICES

APPENDIX ONE
The International Phonetic Alphabet (IPA)

<u>VOWELS</u>
[i] fee
[I] fit
[e] fade
[ε] fed
[ae] fat
[a] flask
[ɑ] far
[ɔ] fog
[o] fold
[u] fool
[ʌ] up (stressed)
[ə] about (unstressed)
[ɜ] fur (stressed)
[ɚ] upper (unstressed)

CONSONANTS

VOICED:
[b] bill
[g] gold
[d] doe
[v] veal
[z] zag
[ʒ] vision
[d] judge
[ð] though

UNVOICED:
[p] pill
[c, k] cold
[t] toe
[f] feel
[s] sag
[ʃ] shy
[tʃ] chat
[θ] thought

<u>NASALS ("CONTINUANTS")</u>
[m], [n]

<u>SEMI-VOWELS ("GLIDES")</u>
[j] piano
[w] everyone, hour

<u>DIPHTHONGS</u>
[ɑi] lie
[ɑu] loud
[e i] lay
[ɔi] loin
[ou] low

APPENDIX TWO
Vowels and Diphthongs

TONGUE VOWELS

I.   From high tongue to flat tongue

2.   From tense tongue to lax

3.   From front tongue to back tongue

Closed Lips   Open Lips

[i]	[I]	[e]	[ε]	[ae]	[a]
bead	bid	bade	bed	bad	bask
(long)	(short)	(long)	(short)	(long)	(short)

Tense Tongue   Lax Tongue
High Larynx   Low Larynx

LIP VOWELS

1.   From tightly rounded lips to relaxed lips

2.   From closed rounded lips to open lips

---

[u]	[U]	[o]	[ɔ]	[ɑ]	[a]
boom	book	bold	ball	bought	bar
long)	(*short*)	(long)	(*short*)	(long)	(*short*)

Note that any vowels that are deeper have longer duration. Short vowels are more clipped and are usually followed by an unvoiced consonant.

CENTRAL VOWELS

[ə]	[ʌ]	[ɚ]	[ɜ]
about	up	upper	purr
unstressed	stressed	*unstressed*	stressed
Tongue neutral	Tongue flat	Tongue forward	Tongue curled
Jaw neutral	Jaw dropped	Jaw forward	Jaw Forward

DIPHTHONGS

A diphthong is a vowel with a changing resonance. Specifically, diphthongs are composed of two elements, the *sustained vowel* and the *vanishing vowel*. Common diphthongs in English include:

In the "tongue diphthong," the vanishing vowel is formulated principally by movement of the tongue tip (for an [j] semivowel, which sounds like a "y"). In the "lip diphthong," the lips adjust for the vanishing vowel, modifying with a [u] (which sounds like a "wuh").

Within the context of a song the diphthongs can be tricky, because anticipation of the vanishing vowel can introduce jaw or tongue tension. The shift in resonance can also effect placement, intonation, and timbre owing to the alteration in vocal tract and hence spectral energy.

Some regional accents are characterized by exaggerated drawls and diphthongs. For instance, excessive jaw, tongue, and lip movements have been associated with the Texas drawl, as well as other Southern drawls. In some states, such as Georgia and Tennessee, speech patterns exhibit tongue tension, while in other southern states such as Alabama, accents incorporate a lax, flat tongue. In the Northeast, the accent is characterized by the *absence* of tongue-tip activity, resulting in tension due to the overcompensation by the mouth and lips. Examples can be found in the classic "park the car," as well as in the absence of the "r" in words like "nervous" or "serve."

APPENDIX THREE
The Categorization of Consonants

NAME		HAVING TO DO WITH...
1.	Fricatives	Friction
2.	Plosives or Stops	Stopping, then exploding
3.	Labials	The Lips
4.	Velars	The Velum
5.	Palatals	The Palate
6.	Dental	The Teeth
7.	Alveolars	Gum ridge behind teeth
8.	Glides or Semi-vowels	Vowel-like consonants
9.	Lingual	The tongue
10.	Voiced or Liquid	Vibration of folds
11	Unvoiced	No vocal fold vibration

TITLE	POINT OF CONTACT	UNVOICED	VOICED
PLOSIVES:	Velar	[k]	[g]
	Palatal	* [tʃ] (chat)	[dʒ] (judge)
	Alveolar	[t]	[d]
	Bi-labial	[p]	[b]
FRICATIVES:	Palatal	[ʃ]	[ʒ]
	Alveolar	[s]	[z]
	Labio-dental	[f]	[v]
	Dental	[θ] (thought)	[ð] (though)
NASALS:	Velar		[ŋ]
	Alveolar		[n]
	Labial		[m]
GLIDES:	Palatal Glide ("Continuant")	[r]	
	Lingual ("Semi-Vowel")		[ɟ]
	Labial	[hw] ("who")	[w]
LATERAL	Alveolar		[l]

*These are also referred to as *affricates* (stop the friction)

REFERENCES

Vibrato

Horii, Yoshiyuki. "Acoustic Analysis of Vocal Vibrato: A Theoretical Interpretation of Data." *Journal of Voice* 3, no. 1 (1989): 36–43.

Kerr, Anita. *Choral Arranging*. New York: MCA Music, 1972.

Large, John. "An Air Flow Study of Vocal Vibrato." *The Voice Foundation: Transcripts of the Eighth Symposium on Care of the Professional Voice* (1979): 39–45.

Large, J., and S. Iwata. "Aerodynamic Study of Vibrato and Voluntary 'Straight Tone' Pairs in Singing." *Folia Phoniatrica* 23 (1971): 50–65.

Mason, Robert M., and Willard Zemlin. "The Phenomenon of Vocal Vibrato." *NATS Bulletin* 22 (1966):12–17.

Radocy, R. E., and J. David Boyle. *Psychological Foundations of Musical Behavior*. Springfield, IL: Charles C. Thomas, 1979.

Rothman, Howard B. "Vibrato: What Is It?" *NATS Journal* (March/April 1984): 16–19.

Seashore, Carl D. *Psychology of Music*. New York: Dover, 1967.

Shipp Thomas, E. Thomas Doherty, and Stig Hagland. "Physiological Factors in Vocal Vibrato Production." *Journal of Voice* 4, no. 4 (1990): 300–304.

Shipp, Thomas, E. Thomas Doherty, and Jean Hakes. "Mean Frequency of Vocal Vibrato Relative to Target Frequency." *Journal of Voice* 3, no. 1 (1989): 32–35.

Smith, Michael. "The Effect of Straight Tone Feedback on the Vibrato." *NATS Bulletin* 28 (May/June 1972): 28–32.

Zemlin, Willard R., Robert M. Mason, and Lisa Holstead. "Notes on the Mechanics of Vocal Vibrato." *NATS Bulletin* 27 (March 1971): 22–26.

Belting

Bevan, Ronald Verle. "Belting and Chest Voice: Perceptual Differences and Spectral Correlates." EdD diss., Teachers College, Columbia University, 1989.

Boardman, Susan D. "Singing Styles on Broadway." *NATS Journal* 45, no. 4 (1989): 4–20.

———. "Vocal Training for a Career in Musical Theater: Pedagogical Goals." *NATS Journal* 48, no. 4 (1992): 11–13, 51.

————. "Vocal Training for a Career in Musical Theater: A Review of the Literature." *NATS Journal* 48, no. 5 (1992): 11–14, 42.

————. "Vocal Training for a Career in Musical Theater: A Pedagogy." *NATS Journal* 49, no. 1 (1993): 8–15, 46–49.

Edwin, Robert. "The Back to Rock Connection: A Pedagogical Perspective." *NATS Journal* 44 (1988): 32–33.

Estill, Jo. "Observations about the Quality Called Belting. In *Transcripts of the Ninth Symposium: Care of the Professional Voice,* Part 2, ed. Van Lawrence. New York: Voice Foundation, 1980.

————. "Belting and Classic Voice Quality: Some Physiological Differences." *Medical Problems of Performing Artists* 3 (March 1988): 37–43.

Hollien, H., W. S. Brown, Jr., and K. Hollien. "Vocal Fold Length Associated With Modal, Falsetto, and Varying Intensity Phonations." *Folia Phoniatrica* 23 (1971): 66–78.

Lawrence, Van. "Laryngological Observations on Belting." *Journal of Research in Singing* 2 (January 1979): 26–28.

Lebon, Rachel L. "The Effects of a Pedagogical Approach Incorporating Video-taped Demonstrations on the Development of Female Vocalists' 'Belted' Vocal Technique." Dissertation Abstracts International, 1986.

Miles, Beth, and Harry Hollien. "Wither Belting?" *Journal of Voice* 4 (1990): 64–70.

Osborne, Conrad D. "The Broadway Voice. Part 1: Just Singing in the Pain." *High Fidelity* 29 (1979): 56–65.

————. "The Broadway Voice. Part 2: Just Singing in the Pain." *High Fidelity* 29 (1979): 57–65.

Rogers, Earl. "To Belt or Not to Belt . . . That is the Question." *NATS Bulletin* 26 (October 1969): 19–21.

Sable, Barbara Kinsey. "The Lilt of Language." *NATS Journal* 47, no. 5 (1991): 10–13.

Schutte, Harm K., and Donald G. Miller. "Belting and Pop, Nonclassical Approaches to the Female Middle Voice: Some Preliminary Considerations." *Journal of Voice* 7, no. 2 (1993): 142–150.

Sullivan, Jan. "How to Teach the Belt/Pop Voice." *Journal of Research in Singing* 13 (December 1989): 41–58.

Sundberg, Johan. "Breathing Behavior During Singing." *NATS Journal* 49, no. 3 (1993): 44–49, 49–51.

Toms, John. "Extensity: A Tonal Concept for Choral Conductors." *Music Educators Journal* (December 1985): 16–18.

Microphone

Clifford, M. *Microphones,* 2d ed. Blue Ridge Summit, PA: Tab Books, 1982.

Nesbitt, A. *Use of Microphones,* 2d ed. Boston: Focal Press, 1983.

Pleasants, Henry. *The Great American Popular Singers.* New York: Simon & Schuster, 1974.

Woram, J. M. *The Recording Studio Handbook.* Plainview, NY: ELAR Publishing, 1982.

————. *The Recording Studio Handbook,* 2d ed. New York: Sams Publishing, 1992.

ANNOTATED BIBLIOGRAPHY

Speech and Science Sources

Aronson, A. E. *Voice Disorders.* New York: Thieme-Stratton, 1980.

Well organized and clear. Especially noteworthy is the author's personal account of his experiences while suffering from a bout with laryngitis, enabling him to more fully appreciate the frustrations and difficulties of his patients first-hand.

Brodnitz, Friedrich. *Vocal Rehabilitation,* 4th ed. Rochester, MN: Custom Printing, 1971. (Paperback: Boston: College Hill Press, 1988.)

This work by one of the pioneers of vocal rehabilitation continues to be cited for its fundamentals and has stood the test of time.

Cooper, Morton. *Modern Techniques of Vocal Rehabilitation.* Springfield, IL: Charles C. Thomas, 1974.

Somewhat outdated but contains some simple and practical suggestions for vocal hygiene and the acquisition of healthy speech patterns. This and subsequent books by this author are also easily understood by the nonprofessional speaker/singer.

Denes P. B., and E. N. Pinson. *The Speech Chain: The Physics and Biology of Spoken Language.* Garden City, NY: Anchor Press/Doubleday, 1973.

As the title implies, this work is still cited as one of the more thorough discussions of language relative to physiology and acoustics as well as linguistic fundamentals.

Eisenson, Jon. *Voice and Diction: A Program for Improvement,* 5th ed. New York: Macmillan, 1985.

A clear, concise, and thorough book on the nature of speech as well as containing a well-designed program for "effective vocalization." Discussion of American speech patterns as well as their evolution; also deals with prosody as well as clear and healthy articulatory patterns. Can be used as a self-study guide.

Luchsinger, R., and G. Arnold. *Voice–Speech–Language.* Belmont, CA: Wadsworth Publishing, 1965.

Broad in scope. Research conducted by these authors is still found in current bibliographies.

Punt, Norman A. *The Singer's and Actor's Throat,* 3d ed. London: Heinemann Medical Books, Ltd, 1979.

Speech handbook that is short and concise regarding voice disorders and their remedies.

Sataloff, Robert Thayer. *Professional Voice: The Science and Art of Clinical Care.* New York: Raven Press, 1991.

A compilation of articles for the National Association of Teachers of Singing (NATS) discussing health issues related to the vocal mechanism. Becomes a medically oriented, comprehensive, and detailed text on the maintenance and care of the professional voice.

Zemlin, Willard R. *Speech and Hearing Science,* 2d ed. Englewood Cliffs, NJ: Prentice-Hall, 1981.

A medical text focusing on the anatomy and physiology of speech and hearing. Contains photographs of organs in situ as well as detailed descriptions of function.

Vocal Pedagogy Sources

Appelman, Ralph D. *The Science of Vocal Pedagogy.* Bloomington: Indiana University Press, 1974.

One of the first voice teachers to advocate a pedagogical approach to singing based on research in anatomy, physiology, and acoustics rather than relying solely on imagery and proprioceptive response.

Bunch, Meribeth. *Dynamics of the Singing Voice.* New York: Springer-Verlag, 1982.

Especially interesting for its mechanistic approach and strong illustrations. Covers a wide range of aspects of vocal pedagogy.

Burgin, J. C. *Teaching Singing.* Metuchen, NJ: Scarecrow Press, 1971.

Observations on teaching voice by using a traditional, empirical approach.

Fields, Victor A. *Foundation of the Singer's Art.* New York: Vantage Press, 1977. (Reprint: NATS Publications, 1984.)

A report summary based on a survey of voice teachers regarding issues in vocal pedagogy, including breath management, the soft-palate positioning, register concepts, tone placement and tone focus, etc.

Miller, Richard. *The Structure of Singing.* New York: Schirmer, 1986.

A combination of the scientific and empirical approaches to vocal pedagogy as described by one of the world's foremost voice teachers. Technical exercises and concepts based on years of teaching plus scientific and acoustical measurements in research. Contains comprehensive bibliography and glossary of musical and nonmusical terms. Used as a vocal-pedagogy text at a number of universities.

Ried, Cornelius. *Voice: Psyche and Soma.* New York: Ralph Patelson Music House, 1965.

A highly regarded book containing insightful observations by a distinguished New York voice teacher, taking a holistic approach to the singing art.

Rushmore, Robert. *The Singing Voice.* New York: Red Dembner Enterprises Corp., 1984.

Interesting aesthetic observations on the singing voice, particularly in terms of timbre and characterization.

Sundberg, Johan. *The Science of the Singing Voice.* Dekalb: Illinois University Press, 1987.

Acoustically oriented scientific approach used in describing the human voice by one of the foremost voice scientists.

Vennard, William. *Singing: The Mechanism and Technic.* New York: Carl Fischer, 1967.

One of the favored texts for vocal pedagogy to the present day, particularly if supplemented with current research and current publications. Discusses anatomy and physiology as it relates to the singing voice specifically. Much of the data derived from landmark research conducted by Vennard himself in conjunction with other well-known scientists and researchers. Contains what might be considered the most comprehensive thesaurus on vocal and musical terms available.

INDEX

abdominal cavity, 4
abduction, 5
accent
    agogic, 119
    tonic, 119
actuator, 3
adduction, 5
aerodynamics, 6
Afro-American influences, 91, 110
alignment, 22
alveolar ridge, 11, 135
ambient noise, 23
amplitude, 9
approximate (vocal folds), 4, 6
articulation, 10–18, 21, 98–100, 122
    jazz articulation, 89
articulators, 4, 10
aspirate attack, 16
attack in phonation, 15, 21, 120
auditions, 72–78
    accompanist, 75–76
    auditioning material, 78
    ballad, 74, 75
    belter, 75
    "legit"or "semi-legit," 75
    patter or up-tempo, 75
    16-bar selection, 74
    tips on auditioning, 78
    "triple threat," 73

belt-mix voice, 116
belting, 109–24

danger signals, 123–24
definition, 111–13
descriptions
    acoustical, 114–15
    physiological, 115
    qualitative, 115
    registration, 115
in musical theatre, 110, 124
in pop-music styles, 110, 111
objectives of pedagogy, 118, 123
prototypical belters, 112
repertoire, 108
spot-checking, 124
vocal quality, 113
Bernoulli effect, 7
"bleat" vibrato, 101
"bracing," 121
breath management, 21
    "bouncing the breath," 56, 120
    breath capacity, 21
    breath pressure, 4
    breath stream, 4
    clavicular breathing, 15
    exercises, 93
    within the speaking voice, 92–93
breath pulse, (breath pulsing,) 120, 121, 123
breath release. *See* releases
breath slur, 91
    exercises, 91
"bridge" of the voice. *See* passagio

ABOUT THE AUTHOR

RACHEL L. LEBON has sung all over the world, including a State Department tour of the former Soviet Union and Portugal as well as a tour with the U.S. Air Force "Tops in Blue," where she performed for troops throughout the United States, Alaska, Hawaii, and the Aleutian Islands as well as in Southeast Asia. She has also done extensive club and studio work, as well as some network television work, in the Dallas/Ft. Worth Metroplex, in Nashville, and throughout Florida. Within the classical realm, she has been actively performing recitals and doing oratorio work, including premiers of works by contemporary composers. She holds Bachelor's and Master's degrees from the University of North Texas (formerly North Texas State University) and a doctorate degree from the University of Miami, and is presently Associate Professor (Jazz Voice) at the University of Miami. She is a member of the Professional Voice Institute, an interdisciplinary team devoted to the treatment of voice disorders. She is an active clinician worldwide, and her articles have been published in the *Journal of the National Association of Teachers of Singing*. Dr. Lebon takes the greatest pride in her students, who have or are currently performing on Broadway, world tours, cruise ships, have recorded, and are teaching, thereby sharing their music and talent throughout the world.